First Published - 1996

Reprinted - 2018

ISBN: 978-81-7141-336-2

Quality Education

Published by:

COVERY PUBLISHING HOUSE PVT. LTD.

4383/4B, Ansari Road, Darya Ganj

New Delhi-110 002 (India)

Phone: +91-11-23279245, 43596064-65

Fax: +91-11-23253475

E-mail: discoverypublishinghouse@gmail.com

sales@discoverypublishinggroup.com

web: www.discoverypublishinggroup.com

Printed at:

Infinity Imaging Systems

Delhi

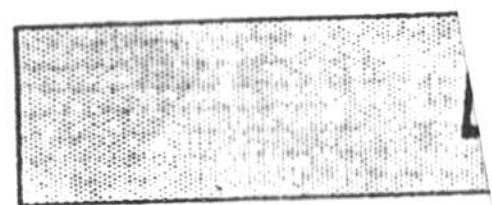

QUA

U K SINGH •

DIS

DISCOVERY PUBLI
NEW DELHI-

Preface

The *DPH Education Handbook* has been created to provide access to information about contemporary topics in education. Practitioners and students at all levels in education have a need to know what is happening today, in addition to historical treatments within the literature.

Each chapter within the Handbook is designed to provide the user with needed "state-of-the-art" information as well as further sources of information. One of the significant features of each chapter is the inclusion of specific programmes, projects and activities so that the researcher can locate human resources as well as the literature.

The handbook will be of use to graduate and post graduate students in education and to practicing teachers, administrators, librarians and planners. The chapters and the further sources of information cited in each book should lead the reader to thousands of people and documents for either research or programme planning purposes.

An effort to achieve universal and effective education is based on a recognition of the rights of students to basic education that enables them to thrive in a complex society, as well as a realization the technological and economic growth is facilitated by increasing the numbers of students, even those with poor academic progresses, who are, in fact successful in learning. Thus, recent and current efforts improve education serve both private and social interests.

This series is addressed to administrators, planners and educators working in the field of education and training with a view to stimulating interest and attention in the areas of education and its related fields. It is also addressed to a growing number of teachers and instructors who will be practitioners in education and who will need to be acquainted with the modern aspects of educational practice and development. Many ideas, generalisations and discussions presented in this series should also prove useful to employing organisations committed to provide training facilities within their establishments—leading to effective mutual participation by institutions and organisations.

The editors wishes to thank the contributors, as well as those organizations that gave permission to publish their extracts, chapters etc.

Editors

Contents

1 Total Quality Management in the Educational Context

TQM - some of the misconceptions

Before defining the elements of TQM if may be useful to say a few words about what TQM is not an imposition. It cannot be done to you or for you. For TQM to work an institution must itself want to introduce it. It is not inspection. It is about always trying to do things right first time and every time, rather than occasionally checking if they have gone wrong. TQM is not about working to someone else's agenda, unless the agenda has been specified by your customers and clients. It is not something which only senior managers do and then pass their directions down the line. The 'total' in TQM dictates that everything and everybody in the organization is involved in the enterprise of continuous improvement. The 'management' in TQM likewise means everyone, because everyone in the institution, whatever their status, position or role, is the manager of their own responsibilities. This is a difficult idea to put across, and it is the reason why some organizations talk, as Rolls-Royee do, about Total Quality rather than TQM.

TQM programmes do not have to use the initial

TQM. Many organizations pursue the philosophy under their own brand name. Boots the Chemist calls its extensive quality programme 'Assured Shopping'. American Express use the initials AEQL, which stands for American Express Quality Leadership. They prefer to emphasize 'leadership' rather than management. Total Quality Control, Total Quality Service, Continuous Improvement, Strategic Quality Management, Systematic Improvement, Quality First, Quality Initiatives, Service Quality are some of the many titles used to describe what in this book is called TQM. If a school, for example, felt that it wanted to call its initiative 'Pupils First' or 'The School Improvement Programme' then it should feel free to do so. It is not the name which is important, but the effect which the quality programme will have on the culture of the school. The pupils and their parents will be interested in the change it brings.

TQM is used to describe two slightly different but related notions. The first is a philosophy of continuous improvement. The second related meaning uses TQM to describe the tools and techniques, such as brainstorming and force-field analysis described in Chapter 10, which are used to put quality improvement into action. TQM is both a mind-set and a set of practical activities - an attitude of mind as well as a method of promoting continuous improvement.

Continuous improvement

TQM is a practical but strategic approach to running an organization which focuses on the needs of its customers and clients. It aims to reject any outcome other than excellence. TQM is not a set of slogans, but a deliberate and systematic approach to achieving appropriate levels of quality in a consistent fashion which meet or exceed the needs and wants of customers. It can be thought of as a philosophy of never-ending improvement only achievable by and through people.

As an approach, TQM seeks a permanent shift in an institution's focus away from short-term expediency to the long-term quality improvement. Constant innovation, improvement and change are stressed, and those institutions which practise it lock into a cycle of continuous improvement. They make a conscious attempt to analyse what they are doing and plan to improve it. To create a continuous improvement culture managers have to trust their staff and to delegate decisions to the appropriate level to give staff the responsibility to deliver quality within their own sphere. Staff need the freedom to operate within a framework of clear and known corporate goals.

'Kaizen'

TQM is accomplished by a series of small-scale incremental projects. The Japanese have a word for this approach to continuous improvement: *kaizen*. This is most easily translated as step-by-step improvement. The philosophy of TQM is large-scale, inspirational and all-embracing, but its practical implementation is small-scale, highly practical and incremental. Drastic intervention is not the means of change in TQM. Grandiose schemes are not the way forward, because often they founder for lack of resources, and their demise can breed cynicism and discontent.

The essence of *kaizen* is small projects which seek to build success and confidence, and develop a base for further ventures in improvement. By way of illustration Joseph Juran talks of 'elephant-sized' and 'bite-sized' projects. He argues that the best way to tackle the 'elephant-sized' projects is to divide them up into manageable 'bit-sized' assignments. He recommends assigning one team the task of 'cutting-up the elephant'. Solid and lasting change is based on a long series of small and achievable projects. It is necessary to work through the activities of the institution very carefully, process by process, issue by issue. Over a period of time more is achieved this way than by trying to make large-scale changes. The incremental approach to quality improvement means that implementation need not be an expensive process. Spending money by itself does not produce quality, although when it is carefully targeted in helps.

A change of culture

TQM requires a change of culture. This is notoriously difficult to bring about and takes time to implement. It requires a change of attitudes and working methods. The staff in institutions need to understand and live the message if TQM is to make an impact. However, culture change is not only about changing the behaviour of staff. It also requires a change in the way in which institutions are managed and led. The latter is characterized by an understanding that people produce quality. Two things are required for staff to produce quality. First, staff need a suitable environment in which to work. They need the tools of the trade and they need to work with systems and procedures which are simple and which aid them in doing their jobs. The environment that surrounds staff has a profound effect on their ability do their job properly and effective. Among the important environmental features are the systems and procedure with which they work. Laying down good and workable procedures by itself does not produce quality, but if procedures are poor or misleading it makes producing quality extremely difficult. Second, to do a good job staff need encouragement and recognition of their successes and achievements. They need leaders who can appreciate their achievement and coach them to greater success. The motivation to do a good job comes from a leadership style and an atmosphere which heightens self-esteem and empowers the individual.

The upside-down organization

The key to a successful TQM culture is an effective internal/external customer-supplier chain. Once the concept has been grasped it has enormous implications for the organization and the relationships within it. The first casualty is the traditional notion of organizational status. The role of senior and middle management in a TQM culture is to support and empower the teaching and support staff and the learners, not to control them. This can most graphically be illustrated by a comparison of the traditional hierarchical organizational chart with its TQM counterpart. The inverted hierarchy is adapted from the ideas of Karl Albretcht. It seeks to illustrate the paradigm shift implicit in TQM. In education it changes the usual set of relationships to one with a clear customer focus. The upside-down organizational focus does not affect the structure of authority in the school or college, and neither does it diminish the essential leadership role of senior managers. In fact, leadership is pivotal to the success of TQM, the inverted hierarchy emphasizes service-giving relationships and the importance of the customer to the institution.

Keeping close to the customers

The primary mission of a TQM institution is to meet the needs and wants of its customers. Excellent organizations, both public and private, keep 'close to the customer', in the words of Peters and Waterman, and have an obsession with quality. They recognize that growth and long-term survival come from matching their service to customer needs. Quality must be matched to the expectations and requirements of customers and clients. Quality is what the customer wants and not what the institution decides is best for them without customers there is no institution.

A customer focus is, however, not by itself a sufficient condition for ensuring total quality. TQM organizations need fully worked out strategies for meeting their customers' requirements. Education faces a considerable challenge in its relationships with its external customers. Many customers are often initially uninformed both about the service and what constitutes its quality. Additionally, expectations are diverse and often contradictory. The quality of particular programmes is often confused in the public mind with the reputation of the institution. Learners' perceptions of quality change as they progress through the institution and their experience and confidence grows.

A further difficulty is that education's customers play an important role in the quality of their own learning. The customers have a unique function in determining the quality of what they receive from education. There are difficulties with notions of consistency in the interactive process of learning. To overcome some of these problems it is necessary to ensure the motivation of both the learners and the staff who serve them. It is also important to making clear what is being offered and what is expected of learners.

Colleagues as customers

The customer focus aspect of TQM does not just involve meeting the requirements of the external customers. Colleagues within the institution are also customers, and rely upon internal services of others to do their job effectively. Everyone working in a school, college or university is both a supplier of services and a customer of others. Each member of staff both gives and receives services. Internal customer relationships are vitally important if an institution is to function efficiently and effectively. The best way of developing the internal customer focus is to help individual members of staff to identify the people to whom they provide services. This is known as the 'next-in-line analysis' and revolves round the following questions:

- Whom do you primarily provide a service to?
- Who relies upon what you do to do their job properly?

The people next-in-line are your direct customers, whether they are external to the institution or internal to it. It is important to find out what they want and to have a good idea of the standards they require. The standards may be contractual, but they may also be negotiable. Notions of status and hierarchy do not enter into this relationship. The standard of service provided to someone junior in the institution is as important as the service provided to the Head teacher, the Principal, or the Chair of Governors.

Internal marketing

It is staff who make the quality difference. They produce successful courses and satisfied clients. Internal marketing is a useful tool for communicating with staff to ensure they are kept informed about what is happening in the institution and have the opportunity to feed back ideas. Simply, the idea of internal marketing is that new ideas, products and services have to be as effectively marketed to staff as they are to clients. Staff cannot convey the message of the institution to potential customers without proper product knowledge and an enthusiasm for the institution's aims. Internal marketing is a stage on from communicating ideas. It is a positive and proactive process which demands a commitment to keep staff informed and to listen to their comments.

Professionalism and the customer focus

There is also the additional dimension of a professional workforce in education who have traditionally seen themselves as the guardians of quality and standards. TQM's emphasis on the sovereignty of the customer may cause some conflict with traditional professional concepts. This a difficult area, and one that will need to be considered by any educational institution taking a total quality route. Training for teachers in quality concepts and thinking is an important element in the required culture change. Staff need to understand how they and their pupils and students will benefit from a change to a customer focus. Total quality is about more than being 'nice to customers and smiling'. It is about listening and entering into a dialogue about peoples' fears and aspirations. The best aspects of the professional role are about care and high academic and vocational standards. Blending the best aspects of professionalism with total quality is essential to success.

The quality of learning

Education is about people learning. If TQM is to have relevance in education it needs to address the quality of the learners' experience. Unless it does that it will not make a substantial contribution to quality in education. In a period when most institutions are being asked to do more with less it is important that they focus on their prime activity - learning.

Learners are all different and learn best in a style suited to their needs and inclinations. An educational institution which takes the total quality route must take seriously the issue of learning styles and needs to have strategies for individualization and differentiation in learning. The learner is the primary customer, and unless the learning style meets individual requirements it will not be possible for that institution to claim that it has achieved total quality.

Educational institutions have an obligation to

make learners aware of the variety of learning methods available to them. They need to give learners opportunities to sample learning in a variety of different styles. Institutions need to understand that many learners also like to switch and mix-'n'-match styles and must try to be sufficiently flexible to provide choice in learning. Miller, Dower, and Inniss make the same point in *Improving Quality in Further Education*. Their argument, which applies to any other type of institution, is that the FE college should 'ensure that learners experience a range of teaching and learning styles so that their chance of success is maximised,.

Much work has still to be done on how to use TQM principles in the classroom. Some of the elements might involve the following pattern. A start could be made with the learners and their teachers establishing their 'mission', which could take the form of 'All Shall Succeed'. From this, negotiation might take place about how the two parties will seek to achieve the mission - the styles of learning and teaching and the resources they require. Individual learners may negotiate their own action plans to give them motivation and direction. The process of negotiation may require the establishment of a quality steering committee or forum to provide feedback and to give the learners an opportunity to manage their own learning. Parents or employers might will be represented on it. Detailed monitoring through progress charting will need to be undertaken by both teachers and students to ensure that all are on track. This is important to ensure that timely and appropriate corrective action can be applied if there is a danger of failure.

The establishing of a strong feedback loop is an important element of any quality assurance process. Evaluation should be a continuous process and not just left until the end of the programme of study. The results of evaluation processes should be discussed with the students, perhaps by means of completing a record of achievement. The very act of being involved in evaluation will assist in building up the students' analytical skills.

It is important that the institution uses the results of the formal monitoring to establish the validity of its programmes. It must be prepared to take the necessary corrective action if the customers' experiences do not meet their expectations. None of this is easy as teachers who have pioneered such processes know. It can be an emotional experience and one that can take unexpected turns. What it does is to provide students with motivation and the practical experience of the use of TQM tools which are transferable to other situations.

Barriers to be overcome when introducing TQM

TQM is hard work. It takes time to develop a quality culture. By themselves hard work and time are two of the most formidable blocking mechanisms to quality improvement. TQM needs a champion in the face of the myriad of new challenges and changes facing education. Quality improvement is a fragile process. All major changes are, Cultures are essentially conservative and homeostasis is the norm. Most staff are most comfortable with what they know and understand. However, to stand still while competitors are improving is a recipe for failure.

If TQM is to work it must have the long-term devotion of the senior staff of the institution. They must back it and drive it. Senior management may themselves be the problem. They may want the results which TQM can bring, but be unwilling to give it their wholehearted support. Many quality initiatives falter because senior managers quickly return to traditional ways of managing. Fear by senior managers of adopting new methods and approaches is a major barrier. This is potentially the most serious of blockages. If senior management do not give TQM their backing there is little that anyone else in the organization can do.

The sheer volume of external pressures also stands in the way of many organizations attempting TQM. Although quality programmes are introduced with considerable publicity, too often they can be overtaken and submerged by other initiatives. There is a need to ensure that despite other pressures quality always has an important place on the agenda. This is where strategic planning plays such an important role.If TQM is firmly a part of the strategic role of the institution, and if there are good monitoring mechanisms in place, then there is a good chance that quality will keep a high profile. This makes it harder to ignore, and increases the chances of its being taken seriously.

The strategic plan can help staff understand the institution's mission. It helps to bridge gaps in communication. There is a need for staff to know where their institution is going and how it will be different in the future. Senior management must trust their staff sufficiently to share their vision for the institution's future. Visions are often not shared because of a fear of a loss of status and disempowerment by managers. When coupled with a fear of delegation by managers this can make quality development nearly impossible. Managers have to be able to let their staff take decisions and be willing to see them make honest mistakes.

A potential problem area in many institutions is the role played in it by middle management. They have a pivotal role because they both maintain the day-to-day operation of the institution and act as one of its most important communications channels. They can often block changes if they have a mind to or they can act as the leaders of teams spearheading the impetus for quality improvement. Middle managers may not define their role as one of innovation unless senior managements communicate to them their vision of a new future. Senior managers must be consistent in their behaviour when advocating and communicating the message of quality improvement. They cannot say on thing and do another and then expect to engender enthusiasm among their staff or loyalty and commitment in their middle managers. They have to persuade others that new working methods will pay dividends.

Barriers to quality are not the sole prerogative of managers. Many staff fear the consequences of empowerment, especially if this go wrong. They are often comfortable with sameness. They need to have the benefits demonstrated to them. For this reason TQM must avoid being about nothing but jargon and hype. This can easily lead to a loss of interest and to scepticism and cynicism, and to the belief that nothing makes any difference. Many of the barriers to TQM involve an element of fear and uncertainty. Fear of the unknown, of doing things differently, of trusting others, and of making mistakes, are powerful defence and resistance mechanisms. Staff cannot give of their best unless they feel that hey are trusted and their views listened to. Deming argues that it is essential when undertaking the quality revolution to 'drive out fear'.

2 Internal Customer and Supplier Relationships

The principle raison d'etre of a TQM organisation is to ensure that its product/service is fit for its purpose and satisfies customer requirements in order that they will repeat their custom and encourage others to be customers thus ensuring the continuing enterprise of the organisation, hopefully at a substantial profit. Within the education context we know that our principal customers - students - require a good quality education that will fit them for their chosen career. It is the Institution's responsibility therefore, to ensure that courses are fit for that purpose both through the curriculum and delivery. However, Atkinson argues that the focus on the external customer must not be at the expense of ignoring the internal customers and finding out their requirements.

As part of the research into Course Monitoring and Review, interviews were conducted with staff in various functional roles including managers, teachers and administrative/clerical staff. A question about the external customer and internal customer formed part of the semi-structured interview. Whilst everyone understood very clearly who was the external customer(s) - primarily the students (but also employers, the professions, Government) - the concept of an internal customer was not so clearly perceived. However, as Leeds Metropolitan University is not as yet a practising TQM culture this is perhaps not so surprising.

Who is our internal customer/supplier?

John Oakland states that: "The next person who checks [uses] your work will be your customer'.

Like many of the principles of TQM this is very simple to state. It is suggested that the reality is much more complex. The many inputs and outputs to the process of Course Monitoring and Review typically include: employers, validating bodies, professional groups, HMI, external examiners, students, staff, committees, boards, student services, academic standards. These may be said to represent the myriad internal customer and supplier relationships that exist for this process alone. If we superimposed on this the numerous other activities that we are involved with we would see that, whilst some customers and suppliers would be removed, others would be added. Indeed even this list has failed to include those support staff who provide the domestic arrangements for a review.

It could be argued, however, that the customer chains obtaining within HE institutions do not and cannot take such a simple linear form. For instance, a senior administrator in a Faculty works with managers, other administrators and teaching staff. Sometimes our relationship to one or other of these groups is as a supplier and sometimes as a customer. Often they can both be in the same process! An example from my own experience would be: to produce the School Examination Timetable the teaching staff have to supply me with their requirements.

What is suggested by this example therefore is that the notion of internal customer and supplier fails to take into account that these relationships flow in both directions, at least certainly for the administrator who is caught in the middle! This suggestion is not intended to be an argument against the value of establishing internal customers and suppliers and finding out their requirements but to suggest that as we do not work in a production line outfit, a different interpretation is perhaps required. For instance, quality chains may be more appropriately applied on an activity basis as opposed to a role basis shows Figure shows how this interpretation has been applied to the activity of examination timetabling.

EXAM TIMETABLING

	Me as Customer		Me as Supplier	
S	Teachers	Quality of	Awards & Exams	C
U	Service			U
P	Awards & Exams	dependent	Draft/Secretary	S
P		upon		T
L	TT wordprocessed	accuracy		O
I	and	Teaching Staff		M
E		timeliness		E
R		of data.	Students	R
S				S

Internal customers/suppliers of exam timetabling process

This approach helps unravel the complex links of a non-linear chain. Once unravelled we can more easily answer the key questions:

- Who are my customers for this activity?
- What are their requirements?
- Who are my suppliers for this activity?
- What are my requirements?

Performance indicators

The extent to which we do or do not meet requirements is the performance indicator (PI)of the quality of our service in our particular role or function.

Once the internal customer/supplier link is established the next stage is to establish the precise requirements in that relationship. We are probably all too familiar with how the requirements of a particular role or task are so often fogged by expectations on the one hand and assumptions on the other. We have probably all heard and used the expression "But I thought you were supposed to be doing that." When roles and requirements remain undefined it is inevitable that this will happen.

TQM gurus use the expression "right first time" (RFT). If this is the ultimate performance indicator why is it so difficult to achieve, bearing in mind that Performance Indicators (PIs) should be achievable? Is it an appropriate PI given the nature of our tasks and the environments in which we work? The days of tradition and stability are over, replaced by a high-speed culture that is constantly changing, leading to the phenomenon of "grey stress" as we come under pressure to adapt and perform. Does this culture permit the time and space to perform RFT?

Not everyone is convinced that TQM is the best thing since sliced bread. RFT would make all our lives easier - no more redrafting of notices of meetings because you got the date wrong, because you were interrupted by the telephone and someone came to your desk wanting just a quick word; no more redoing the student numbers spread sheet for the nth time because some enrolment forms have been discovered on a staff member's desk three months after enrolment; no more redrafting the Course Document because it has been decided to change the sequence of sections. Yet these events are the realities of our daily lives. Indeed it is as much a part of our service to internal customers, as to external customers, to respond to requests and change. Is RFT not then a rather sanctimonious view of an ivory-tower theorist? Add to this the patronising comments from senior management such as "we never have the time to get it right first time but all have the time to get it right second, third time" and RFT as a PI can really stick in your throat.

What is the nature of this PI and others within our real environment? Are they not in fact a stick with which to threaten rather than motivating objectives? Certainly at the macro level they are used as such by the funding bodies. If objectives and targets are not met then funding is reduced. In this regard PIs take on the quota function of the production line. The answer to these criticisms of course is that it all depends on the culture in which PIs and all the other principles of TQM are applied - the subject of my final section.

Ignoring the arguments against PIs it is contested that they are still a very problematical area for the academic administrator. What sort of PIs could be applied to the administrator?

A few suggestions might be: turnaround time - how long for a specific task?; 24-hour response time for standard information; accuracy; sensitivity to different perspectives; value as an information source; use of secretaries.

For PIs to be realistic and achievable they must be looked at in terms of the internal customer/ supplier relationships and the number of those that exist. If you have a reputation for being good then you attract more customers but how many customers can be realistically and effectively dealt with before the service is reduced and your reputation tails off - as with a busines over-extending itself? It may actually be necessary to reduce customer volume in order to improve quality.

There is another difficulty consequent upon applying PIs in a non-TQ environment. Whilst they may be legitimate to measure the performance of an organisation, in our present culture they become personalised - they become focussed on an individual rather than on the structures/teams in place to support that individual in their activity. Taking account of the above limitations, the reality of our present lives could counter each of the suggested PIs as follows:

turnaround time

- four weeks for an Exam Timetable - what if the Dean wants a breakdown of student numbers by domicile in the meantime?

- 24-hour response time for standard information
- what is standard? If its not in "the book", is it not standard? What happens when the person who can give you the information is away till next Tuesday?
- accuracy
- no argument on this provided we work in an environment that is conducive to concentration and checking
- sensitivity to different perspectives
- how do you measure sensitive?
- value as an information source
- how do you measure value?
- use of secretaries - this is a real one!
- how many times do we send a piece of work back because we have redrafted it as opposed to there being typographical mistakes to be corrected?

Ideally - in a TQM environment - none of these provisos should apply. In the meantime the reality is that they do.

TQM Principles in a non-tq environment

Readers will probably know that TQM is a philosophy which sets out to achieve optimum efficiency and effectiveness by reducing waste and error through the application of certain principles and operating methods to achieve quality in every aspect of an operation to satisfy external customer requirements.

So far I have focused on just two of the

principles/operating methods required for a TQM culture - establishing internal customer/supplier relationships and the use of performance indicators. However desirable, it is suggested that these principles cannot be applied in isolation of an all-encompassing TQ culture. I shall now explore some of the key features that are required for this culture.

Leadership and commitment

Quality is a strategic issue and an attitudinal position. The decision to go down that road must be led by the Senior Managers of an organisation for it is from this level that attitudes in an organisation are inculcated. It is through the example and commitment of Senior Managers to quality that the whole organisation is enabled to adopt a quality ethos.

Resources

The provision of resources for education and training is crucial - to educate people in ways of working in a quality environment and training to practise error prevention rather than error detection; in the use of problem-solving techniques and tools.

Another valuable resource is time - time to do the job RFT. Time management courses may help but consideration also needs to be given to the actual management of staff resources to support the various activities.

Communication

Open communication is a crucial feature of a TQM culture. In order for employees to feel committed to an organisation's objectives they need to know and understand what these are. Decisions are made with regard to objectives - how to implement them, why they might change, how they bear upon an employee's place and operation of work. Employees are the implementation channel through which an objective is met. In a TQM culture, however, communication goes further to become an interactive process leading to participation.

Participation

An organisation may have very good channels of communication - newsletters, up-to-date notice boards, regular policy statements -but if people are not involved in the decision making processes a sense of belonging and commitment is not cultivated. A non-participative style of management perpetuates an "us and them" syndrome. My research showed evidence of this attitude at Leeds Metropolitan University - between teaching staff and management, teaching staff and administrators, administrators and managers.

Each perceived the other group as taking decisions which affected their lives but without reference to them. "Old style" management might consider that it is the prerogative of management to make "managerial decisions". TQM does not sustain this prerogative. Instead it recognises that participation has a lot to do with an individual's sense of power and control. Powerlessness undermines confidence and motivation and does not inspire a sense of responsibility. Participation brings about a sense of involvement, identity and responsibility - for the task and the objective.

Team building

Establishing a culture of open communication and

participation can be a foundation for team building. The value of team building has often been stressed in management handbooks. In TQM, teams may come under the guise of "quality circles", "problem solving teams". Whatever their guise it is suggested that they can achieve more than their purpose at hand if they are cross-functional and/or cross-departmental. They help build on participation and involvement.

These selected basic principles of TQM are in themselves not that original in management theory. But it is the combination of them in a specific context that makes TQM different and so very difficult to achieve. It is difficult to implement because it is a very long term and continuing process, requiring wholehearted commitment and, probably, an initial outlay of resources. More significantly however, it requires a fundamental change to most organisations' corporate culture: from a closed culture that is secretive and dominated by coercion and intimidation, resulting in staff being defensive and non-critical of performance, to an open culture where fear is driven out, barriers broken, targets eliminated. Where people are self-critical and take pride in their workmanship - these are the values which provide the impetus for improvement.

3 Developing Managerial Capabilities in Education

The Background

The major concern in the management literature in the 1980s has been the development of management competences. Since the purpose of the study of management is to improve performance, it is not surprising that attention should be focused on an analysis of what abilities managers need in order to be effective and various categorizations have emerged. The beginnings of the research for generic management competences can be traced back to the 1970s when the American Management Associations (AMA) launched a project based on observation and analysis of 1,800 management jobs.

In the AMA managerial competency model which emerged competence is defined as 'a generic knowledge, motive, trait, self-image, social role, or skill of a person that is causally linked to superior performance on the job'. The model identified, in addition to specific knowledge competence, four clusters of generic competences which they identify as intellectual, entrepreneurial, socio-emotional and interpersonal. In Britain academic study and research was given a marked stimulus by the

Management Charter Initiative (MCI), a large-scale industry-led management development programme supported by central government which now involves over 200 UK leading private and public organizations. A price to be paid for government support, particularly in the British political scene, given the relatively short periods between elections, is that results have to be visible, immediate and measurable. Consequently there has been an inevitable tendency to produce checklists often containing an undifferentiated collection of personal characteristics, mechanistic skills, management processes and much more complex abilities.

In the field of education the growing recognition of the crucial importance of good management practices in school was dramatically strengthened by the impact of 'local management of schools' imposed by the 1988 Education Reform Act. Central government clearly regards management development as a key element in its declared strategy for ensuring improvement in the quality of education to meet the needs of industry and the economy. Fortunately the years that followed the Act have coincided with the period when serious doubts are being expressed about the basic idea of analysing a professional management task into itemized elements of competence. It is increasingly recognized that the overall ability to perform effectively is more than the sum of a set of subordinate abilities. Jacobs makes the point that while it is possible, by obtaining and carefully analysing performance data, to identify clusters of behaviour that can be reliably and logically classified as competences, what is obtained is only a partial and fragmented view of the complexity of management. Management performance involves other activity which is difficult to isolate and describe; it involves qualities and abilities which are not easy to observe or discover; it has outcomes which defy measurement.

The Management Task Force set up by the Secretary of State for Educations to identify and explore some of the issues involved in management development in schools has largely rejected the prescription of training in an arbitrarily determined set of skills as the way forward. This has contributed to a growing conviction that those who manage are in the best position to identify what their needs may be. This approach is reinforced by a current general political philosophy that 'the customer knows best'. Thus the identification of need is a major concern among providers of management development and it is generally held that it is essential for schools to feel ownership of the programmes through being fully and directly involved in planning their content, style and procedures.

The idea that managers themselves are best able to determine their own development needs has a common sense appeal, and the needs of practitioners as they perceive them provides a reasonable starting point in attempting to determine what competences are required and how they might be developed. There are, however, a number of obvious difficulties. Even those strongly committed to full participation by schools in devising education management programmes admit that 'current concerns force an attitude of short termism and coping with immediate practicalities rather than long term planning' (Styan, 1991). Thus it is not surprising that solutions to pressing problems are a need more strongly felt than the search for underlying generic capabilities. Also, it cannot be assumed that practitioners, however wiling, will be able to engage in the diagonistic and analytical process necessary to identify competences associated with effectiveness. The methods required to probe beyond and beneath the easily identifiable daily concerns and practices of managing are likely to be based on rigorous analysis, reflection and debate by practioners and are as yet largely underdeveloped.

The research methodology

In determining an appropriate method of enquiry the researchers were informed from three sources: The Peer Assisted Learning Project of the Far West Laboratory for Education Research and Development, San Francisco.

Effective peer group interaction, an integral part of the action research approach, is the cornerstone of the Master of Science programme at the University of Ulster. Groups are encouraged to engage in reflective enquiry which seeks to analyse and understand their own and others' practice leading to courses of action for sustained improvement. Creative thinking is also encouraged as a complementary activity by which is meant the ability to form novel associations from looking at the elements of managerial reality in an open and unconstrained way. This approach offered the possibility of uncovering, if they existed, elusive generic capabilities from complex realities.

The focus group as a form of qualitative research has many characteristics in common with features of the above approach: 'The hallmark of the focus group is the explicit use of the group interaction to produce data and insights that would be less accessible without the interaction found in a group'. The style of approach is exploratory rather than hypothesis testing and based on interview and interaction. Surprisingly focus groups have not been widely used in research in the social sciences or education, but the method clearly offers a valuable vehicle for group members experienced in rigorous reflective analysis.

For this research six headteachers were chosen from the primary, secondary and further education sectors and two female members were included to allow for possible differences in style and practise. All are alumni of the MSc programme and had the advantage of three years of cognitive development in the group dynamics described above.

The researchers acted as moderators, adopting a detached style which allowed members to raise and explore issues they felt were significant but maintaining proximity to the focus of enquiry. Criteria were identified and applied which governed the quality of interaction, namely, coverage of a board range of matters recognized on significant, precise and detailed accounts, and rigorous searching analysis. The group met on ten occasions during the period June 1988-November 1989. In each of these tape-recorded sessions members were encouraged to identify situation/incidents in their practice, to reflect on the intentions and outcomes of the action taken, and to attempt to distil from their discussions what they perceived to be the capacities necessary for success.

Group deliberations

The constraints of a relatively brief paper prevent a detailed account of each of the ten sessions. As decision-making is the vital element in the managing task two contrasting decision issues are selected as examples. In the account which follows contributors are identified by sector (primary (PS), or secondary (SS), or further education (FE)); status (maintained (M), i.e. Catholic, or state (S)); and gender male (m), or female (f)).

Example 1

During the opening session in Drumcree High School, whether or not to join Education for Mutual Understanding (EMU) was offered as an issue requiring a Yes/No decision within a short time-span. EMU is a major curriculum project in Northern Ireland and is heavily resourced and supported by the Department of Education and the present education minister. It seeks to encourage sympathetic and understanding relationships between Catholic and Protestant schools, However, it has been opposed by many local politicians, churches and community members who see it both as a first step towards integrated schooling and an imposed initiative from central government at Westminster. Everyone in the group regarded it as a critically important decision with clear political overtones as well as educational implications. In two schools in particular the political/community aspects dominated. One school is in a strongly nationalist area seeking to preserve its distinctive Irish culture and identity. Nevertheless the headteacher saw his task as persuading the governors to enter the project. The other school is in a staunch unionist area and the headteacher was well aware that her governors would oppose and political interference they perceived as emanating from Westminster. The EMU issue instigated a lengthy discussion about the tactics that might be used. There was some disagreement over the question of how much direction/information should be given to a board of governors. All concurred that they were able to influence their boards of governors and a vital tactic was the winning of support of keyfigures. All were able to recognize the key figures in their governing bodies and stressed the paramount importance of good relationships with the chairperson. They felt it was also important to know the interests, dispositions and beliefs of all members of the boards of governors.

It was also apparent in this opening session that many of the concepts and capacities identified and sharpened in later group meeting as constituting what managers need to be good at were freely used. Having recognized EMU as a potentially emotive political issue, they saw the capacity to read the situation as critically important: the boar of governors, teacher attitudes, community perceptions, resource implications, reactions of the Department of Education and the area boards were consequential variables in the circumstances. Concepts like balanced judgement, political acumen, judicious caution, and skills like reconnaissance, persuading, negotiating and bargaining recurred in the discussion.

Example 2

Some of the literature on decision-making distinguishes between 'routine' decisions (structured, certain, simple, recurring, standardized) and 'non-routine' decisions (unstructured, uncertain, complex, non-recurring, novel). In one group session the danger of assuming that routine recurring decisions are necessarily simple and certain became apparent. The conclusion was reached that the capable manager is one who has the insight to recognize when apparently simple decisions may have complex undertones.

Discussion had centred on the broad issue of the expected consequence of the new legislation which has been introduced in Northern Ireland in parallel with the Education Reform Act, 1988. One of the group, almost as an aside, posed the question: 'What do we do if a teacher asks for leave of absence not provided for by the regulations? On the face of it this is a routine issue where agreed procedures and required information are readily available.In the case of further education this indeed appears to be so. The FE principal pointed out that his staff have clear contracts and 'it should just be played by the book'. He added, 'Of course, in FE the principal can distance himself from such decisions'. In the primary and secondary sectors the situation is less clear cut. Although regulations governing leave of absence exist, the primary and secondary headteachers felt that strict adherence to such a tight delineation could easily lead to staff also playing by the book. They argued that flexibility was needed but that such flexibility cold create its own potential difficulties and that the exercise of judgement, tact and sensitivity was essential.

The conversation broadened into a fuller discussion of the kinds of relationships between headteacher and teaching staff that characterize effective schools and colleges. Marked differences in attitude and opinion became apparent which partly reflected differences in context but, more markedly, differences in personality and perceptions.In particular the female members emphasized the importance of close, supportive relationships. One of them made the point: "We have introduced counselling for pupils but we seem to neglect the important area of counselling for our staff.' Once again the issue of relationships with staff seemed to hinge on balanced judgement.

Differences between the views of the FE principal and the headteachers in the primary and secondary sectors were revealed: 'The powers of the principal are awesome in the new situation. You are part of the employer. You cannot have a close relationship. You will have to distance yourself from the informal relationships which exist in any college.' The opposing view was most strongly expressed by a female headteacher: 'You cannot step back. You will lose the spirit of the school and its main purposes. You must win the respect of the staff. You have to build bridges and establish relationships with key figures.'

When the attention of the group was directed to the focal issue of what the manager needs to be good at in establishing and maintaining co-operative relationships or, more broadly, in managing people, the usual interpersonal skills were offered - communicating, negotiating, bargaining, influencing, counselling. There were, however, many caveats expressed and there was a general consensus that more fundamental cerebral capacities distinguish the more effective manager from the less effective: thinking on your feet, balanced judgement, assessing the situation.

Summary and conclusions

What emerged from the conversation was a more complex picture than presented in much of the literature on management competence. In the end the group identified three elements that constitute capability:

(1) Knowledge - relevant information relating to the school's context, functions and processes which the manager needs to possess or have ready access to.

(2) Skills - techniques that can be acquired through training and that can be improved through practice.

(3) Higher order capacities - generic cognitive abilities which determine appropriate action.

The proposition which emerges from the investigation is that while knowledge and skills are prerequisite tools in the process of managing a given situation the group strongly argues that it is the higher order capacities which are the vital elements in the process of using knowledge and skills in effective action.

There was common assent on the main areas of knowledge required by senior managers in schools: professional knowledge of educational principles and practices, knowledge of theories and model of management, and knowledge of the social, political and legal contexts. Equally the discrete skills required by managers were generally agreed: persuading, bargaining, explaining, listening, reporting, informing, counselling, appraising, chairing, interviewing, and team building are typical of a list which keeps being added to. Skills have been enumerated in key areas like curriculum, organization and resource management, and development programmes are often predicated on the assumption, often unexamined, that these can be effectively managed through the acquisition of skills that are teachable, learnable and transferable. Few analyses have been made of the nature of the enabling capacities needed to apply skills appropriately in the complex situations in which managers in schools find themselves daily. Since these higher order capacities were deemed by the group to be those which characterized the above average performers, they naturally became the main focus of continuing discussion. The researchers present here the attempt to capture and clarify the ideas which emerged from intense, prolonged discussion involving complex philosophical and psychological issues. The following key higher order capacities were finally identified from a distillation of complex interrelated concepts: reading the situation, balanced judgement, intuition and political acumen.

Reading the situation

This emerged as the overriding capacity and was voiced in a variety of ways: 'picking up the vibes around you'; 'keeping your antennae out'; being aware of other possibilities and options'; able to assess and weigh up all the factors in the situation'; 'being alert and receptive to what is going on'.

It was also seen to apply to a wide range of decision-making circumstances: long-term strategic planning, handling; crisis situations and recurring, daily encounters. The FE principal in particular stressed that sensitive awareness and diagnosis are important in the light of the new legislation and the growing volume of boundary management. The views expressed seemed to recognize that 'reading the situation' involves more than mere diagnosis; it includes continuous response and deliberate action to influence evolving circumstances. The need for action was constantly stressed: 'You need to read the situation as accurately and quickly as possible and be seen to take appropriate action.' Reconnaissance, identification of areas requiring, attention, analysis, reflection, synthesis and evaluation were seen as contributory elements, many of which occur in the other cognitive activities which are identified.

Balanced judgement

The ability to exercise balanced judgement was also seen as critical. Group members saw it as related to problem-solving in that, once a situation has arisen or a problem has been recognized, analysis follows and key factors are identified and evaluated in the process of choosing a course of action. It was clear that as the group distilled their thinking over a number of sessions they did not see it as an exercise in mechanical logic: 'It is not merely clinical analysis but a combination of that with intuition.' There was considerable agreement that the kind of judgement necessary is significantly different from judgement in the legal sense: 'You have to be prepared to base decisions on much softer evidence than would be accepted in a court of law. You very rarely have time to collect all the evidence you would like and you have to exercise judgement on a partial picture. Values also can't be left out of the picture.' The issue of values arose in a number of contexts but particularly in relation to the context created by the new legislation: 'You must be aware of the values you are perceived to embody and perceived to protect.' 'Does school reflect the world out there as it is - or should it project what the world out there might be?'

It is interesting that while many writers speak about making sound judgments the recurring theme in the discussion was about balanced judgement. The group saw the examining and weighting of the advantages and disadvantages of factors in often ambiguous and conflicting circumstances as important and the testing of decisions against the priorities and values of the school. Balanced judgements was seen as particularly important in time of crisis and dilemma.

Intuition

Intuition was seen as serving judgement, following a long debate about the relationships between experience, creative thinking, judgement and intuition. The group did not agree with a conception of intuition as devoid of thought. 'Intuition is more than mere hunch or guesswork. It may start as a gut feeling but is tested against the bank of your own experience.'

Two key elements recurred in the attempt to capture the essence of intuition: the part played by experience and the part played by a thinking process. The groups saw stored memory and ordered experience as important. It is interesting that they independently derived a conception close to that outlined by a number of recent writers, who suggest that the basis of intuition lies in the ability spontaneously to tap the mind's compressed store of experience, knowledge and understanding. A top executive in industry express a view, reported in Vaughan, which would clearly be accepted by members of the group: 'I don't think intuition is som magical thing. I think it is a subconscious drawing from innumerable experiences that are stored. You draw from this reserve without conscious thought.' Similarly, the group perceptions of the role of thinking in intuition are similar to aspects of the concept of creativity developed by a number of writers. Henry regards creativity as 'associated with imagination, insight, invention, motivation, ingenuity, inspiration and intuition'. The cerebral aspects of intuition were constantly stressed by the group.

Political acumen

While political skills have featured prominently in lists of what managers need to be good at, the group make an important distinction between possession of political skills, like bargaining, and political acumen: 'It's not enough to know how to bargain but when to bargain. Timing is all important.' Their notion of political acumen is closely tied in with thinking on one's feet, learning from experience, reading the situation and using intuition: 'It is about hearing what people are not saying. That's part of political awareness.' Thus political awareness has to do with sensitivity and with flexibility to take account of changing situations rather than relying simply on experience: 'You, others and circumstances will have changed.' In discussion of the new legislation the group stressed the importance of such tactics as controlling information, identifying and cultivating key parties, establishing effective networks, developing credibility and occupying pubic space.

Review

In an early session one group number captured the initial feelings about effective headteachers: 'You know who they are but you don't know why they are.' In the final review session the group claimed to have come to a clearer understanding of the 'why'. They felt that while they had greater conceptual clarity it was still difficult to put the essence into words. They seem to confirm the assertion in Pye that managerial behaviour is 'something about which we can know more than we can tell'.

Equally, in the ten sessions there was much more told than can be reported in this brief account. For example, the group saw personal qualities like integrity, stamina, commitment and conviction as fundamental and greater emphasis was placed on the foundation role of value systems than appears in the account.

Phase two

For the second phase of the investigation three headteachers from the original group were retained. Three new members were included who had also successfully completed the MSc in Education Management programme. There was a deliberate widening of group background to include a broader spectrum from education and the health service. In the account which follows contributions are identified as before by sector: primary (P), secondary (S), further education (FE), higher education (HE), area board (equivalent to LEA) (AB), nurse education (NE), and by gender: male (m), or female (f).

Throughout the five sessions held the three key elements of knowledge, skills and higher order capacities identified during the first phase were reconsidered and confirmed: that is, managerial capability is realized in effective action in which knowledge and skills are used appropriately through the exercise of higher order capacities.

The four higher order capacities of reading the situation, balanced judgement, intuition and political acumen were also confirmed throughout the sessions. Creativity was seen as making a vital contribution to the higher order capacities and managerial capability, particularly in times of complex, turbulent change in public and private sector management. Kindred terms like imagination, insight, originality and inventive thinking were seen as appropriate in such times of flux. The group believed that effective management integrated the more systematic analysis, reflection and synthesis implied by classical, rational approaches with creative perspectives which look for new, unanticipated, unexpected ways of seeing, thinking and doing. In this the group are reflecting the new emerging in recent management literature that rational enquiry and on-rational insight should be complementary. Wisdom also appeared as a central concept in the group discussions and there was some debate about what constituted the wise manager. One group member tended to equate wisdom with a degree of caution which inhibits action and creativity but others in the group argued that creativity and risk-taking should be seen as important elements of wise management.

The central concern for the second phase was the question: what are the implications for planning management development programmes? The group felt that much of the thinking on management development failed to distinguish clearly enough between management processes, key management areas and managerial capability. Group members argued for a three-dimensional model which recognized that managerial capability is exercised in key management areas through generic managing processes. There was agreement that in education, as in all organizations, generic management processes can be identified which include deciding, communicating, devising and influencing. The key areas identified in educational institutions were resources, curriculum, organization and administration. with the changing emphasis on competition and accountability external and boundary management were seen as crucial areas. The group argued that management development programmes need to identify the underlying capacities required to be good at these processes in these areas.

The single overriding message that the group stressed in that management development initiatives should develop managerial capability and need to be clearly targeted in their intentions. The three elements of knowledge, skills and higher order capacities clearly interrelate as one group member stated: 'Knowledge, skills and higher order capacities are all interleaving in that knowledge and skills have their contributions to make to higher order capacities. They all influence each other in many ways.' The group emphasized the importance of targeting initiatives both in terms of what is appropriate and in recognition that at different times during a manager's career different balances and kinds of learning are likely to be necessary. Group members also presented the view that all teachers are managers and have significant contributions to make to the health of the organization, particularly in present and future times of large-scale change and turbulence. For education and the health service this implies a change of culture, both within the system and institutions, which rests on openness, trust, sharing and participation by all.

The transmission of required knowledge is relatively straightforward and may be offered in oral, written and visual forms or in combination. Equally, well established procedures for the acquisition of management skills exist through approaches like workshops, social skills training programmes and those employing more sophisticated technology like interactive video. Although not underestimating the importance of acquiring specific and appropriate knowledge and receiving training in management skills, the new group reaffirmed and strongly supported the belief that higher order capacities are the determining factor in effective management action: 'Management is a cluster of skills involving things like influencing, good communication and so forth. It's that but it's much more than that. You can never be fully trained in it.' While they agreed that higher order capacities are needed at all stages in a teacher's career, they argued that they assume increasing importance with promotion. Several members gave examples of teachers who had found difficulty as they progressed.

Much group debate centred on how higher order capacities might be developed. They questioned the usefulness of 'second-hand' experience like simulation exercises in that 'solutions' are more easily arrived at freed from the constraints of a real context. they also felt that facile answers to simulated situations can be accepted when the problems presented are not owned by the participations and therefore concerns of accountability do not arise. they maintained that, while higher order capacities may develop *through experience* there are also ways in which *learning from experience* can be assisted: 'You probably have to learn it on the job but it's more than learning on the job. This is where the group is so important. The sense you make of your own experience results from the group. This has to be related back into your continuing experience.'

Thus the value of sharing and utilizing the breadth of experience and expertise through peer group interaction as has taken place in the focus group was recognized and the group came down heavily in favour of this approach. It developed precisely the kinds of self-analysis, awareness and critical reflection through which the higher order capacities might be developed: the research method becomes the developmental medium. The researchers certainly became aware that the members of the focus group developed both individually and as a group during the course of the research and there were qualitative differences a group during the course of the research and there were qualitative differences in terms of the criteria of range, specificity and depth between initial and later sessions.

However, member emphasized that peer group conversion needs monitoring and guidance. They saw a real danger in sessions becoming anecdotal. The term 'monitor' was used to describe this advisory, guiding role and it was felt that this person should be 'itinerant', that is, outside the group, to avoid the possibility of claustrophobia and lack of breadth likely in a restricted setting. they regarded it as essential that lack of breadth likely in a restricted setting. They regarded it as essential that the mentor should have high credibility as a practitioner and the consultant in the medical world was offered as a pertinent example. The importance of identifying accurately the essential needs of managers was stressed and it was argued that the mentor had a crucial role to play in diagnosing the underlying causes rather than the symptoms, and in recognizing the importance of the lasting and the long-term rather than the immediate and short-term which tend to distort management priorities. Managers with differing backgrounds and experience and in different positions in the organization will require relevant, and indeed individual, development programmes which are tailored to meet their needs. In the final session it was proposed that underpinning the thinking process which are at the heart of effective management is the asking of right questions in an attempt to arrive at appropriate answers. Such questioning and ensuing reflection may be applied to past experience, to present circumstances and to anticipation of the future under the guidance of an experienced, skilled mentor.

It is interesting that the group arrived independently at a conception of management which is similar to that presented in recent literature on creative management. The model that they present as a working tool for planning effective development programmers appears to be worth trying out.

4 Educational Leadership for Quality

The educational leader

Total quality is a passion and a way of life for those organizations who live its message. The question is how to generate the passion and the pride required to generate quality in education. Peters and Austin researched the characteristics of excellence for their book *A Passion for Excellence*. Their research led them to the brief that what makes the difference is leadership. they argue strongly for a particular style of leadership to lead the quality revolution - a style to which they have given the acronym, MBWA or 'management by walking about'. A passion for excellence cannot be communicated from behind the office desk. MBWA emphasizes both the visibility of leaders and their understanding and feeling for the front-line and the processes of the institution. This style of leadership is about communicating the vision and the values of the institution to others, and getting out among the staff and customers and experiencing the service for themselves.

Peters and Austin gave specific consideration to educational leadership in a chapter entitled 'Excellence in School Leadership'. Their prescription of the qualities required of an excellent educational leader are worth consideration. they see the educational leader as needing the following perspectives:

- Vision and symbols. The Headteacher or Principle must communicate the institution's values to the staff, pupils and student and the wider community.
- 'Management by waling about' is the required leadership style for any institution.
- 'For the Kids'. This is their educational equivalent to 'close to the customer'. It ensures that the institution has a clear focus on its primary customers.
- Autonomy, experimentation, and support for failure. Educational leaders must encourage innovation among their staff and be prepared for the failures that inevitably accompany innovation.
- Create a sense of 'family'. The leader needs to create a feeling of community among the institution's pupils, students, parents, teachers, and support staff.
- 'Sense of the whole, rhythm, passion, intensity, and enthusiasm.' These are the essential personal qualities required of the educational leader.

The significance of leadership for undertaking the transformation to TQM should not be underestimated. Without leadership at all levels of the institution the improvement process cannot be sustained. Commitment to quality has to be a top-down process. It has been estimated that 80 per cent of quality initiatives fail in the first two years. The main reason for failure is lack of senior management backing and commitment. Quality improvement is too important to leave to the quality co-ordinator. To succeed in education TQM leave to the quality co-ordinator. To succeed in education TQM requires strong and purposeful leadership.

Typically, managers in non-TQM organizations spend 30 per cent of their time in dealing with systems failure, complaints and with 'fire-fighting'. As TQM saves that time managers have more time to lead, plan ahead, develop new ideas and work closely with customers.

Communicating the vision

Senior management must give the lead and provide vision and inspiration. In TQM organizations all managers have to be leaders and champions of the quality process. They need to communicate the mission and cascade it throughout the institution. Many managers, particularly middle managers, may find total quality difficult to accept and to implement. It involves a change in the management mind-set as well as a change of role. it is a change from the 'I'm in charge' mentality to that of manager as supporter and leader of front-line staff. The function of leadership is to enhance the quality of learning and to support the staff who deliver it. While this sounds obvious it is not always the way management functions are viewed. Traditional notions of status can lie uneasily with the total quality approach. TQM turns the traditional institution on its head and inverts and the hierarchy of functions. It empowers the teachers and can provide them with greater scope for initiative. It is for this reason that it is often said of TQM institutions that they requires less management and more leadership.

The role of the leader in developing a quality culture

What is the role of the leader is an institution undertaking a total quality initiative? No list of attributes says it is all, but the major functions of leadership are as follows. A leader must:

- have a vision of total quality for his or her institution;
- have a clear commitment to the quality improvement process;
- communicate the quality message;
- ensure that customer needs are at the centre of the institution's policies and practices;
- ensure that there are adequate channels for the voices of customers;
- leader staff development;
- be careful not to blame others when problems arise without looking at the evidence. Most problems are the result of the policies of the institution and not the feelings of staff;
- lead innovation within their institutions;
- ensure that organizational structures clearly define responsibilities and provide the maximum delegate compatible with accountability;
- be committed to the removal of artificial barriers whether they be organizational or cultural;

- build effective teams;
- develop appropriate mechanisms for monitoring and evaluating success.

Empowering teachers

A key aspect of the leadership role in education is to empower teachers to give them the maximum opportunity to improve the learning of their students. Stanley Spanbauer, the President of Fox Valley Technical College, who has taken a lead in introducing TQM into vocational education in the USA, argues that 'in quality-based approach, school leadership relies on the empowerment of teachers and others involved in the teaching/learning process. Teachers share in decision-making and assume greater responsibilities. they are given more power to act and greater responsibilities. They are given more power to act and greater autonomy in almost everything they do.' He goes on to elaborate his belief in the importance of leadership with these words: 'Commitment means much more than giving an annual speech on how important quality is to our school. It requires unending enthusiasm and devotion to quality improvement.

Spanbauer has put forward a plan for leadership to create a new educational environment. He argues that educational leaders should guide and assist others to develop a similar set of characteristics. This encourages shared responsibility and a style which will engender an interactive working environment. He visualizes a leadership style where leaders 'must walk and talk quality and understand that change happens by degree, not by decree'. Leaders have a pivotal role in guiding teachers and administrators to work for and in concert with their client groups. Spanbauer is essentially concerned with leadership for empowerment. His conclusions are:

1. Involve teachers and all staff in problem-solving activities, using basic scientific methods and the principles of statistical quality and process control.
2. Ask them how they think about things and how projects can be handled rather than telling them how they will happen.
3. Share as much management information as possible to help foster their commitment.
4. Ask staff which systems and procedures are preventing them from delivering quality to their customers - students, parents, coworkers.
5. Understand that the desire for meaningful improvement of teachers is not compatible with a top-down approach to management.
6. Rejuvenate professional growth by moving responsibility and control for professional development directly to the teachers and technical workers.
7. Implement systematic and continued communication among everyone involved in the school.
8. Develop skills in conflict resolution, problem-solving, and negotiations while displaying greater tolerance for and appreciation of conflict.
9. Be helpful without having all the answers and without being condescending.

10. Provide education in quality concepts and subjects such as team building, process management, customer service, communication, and leadership.
11. Model, by personally exhibiting desired characteristics and spending time walking around, listening to teachers and other customers.
12. Learn to be more like a coach and less like a boss
13. Provide autonomy and allow risk-taking while being fair and compassionate.
14. Engage in the delicate balancing act of ensuring quality to external customers (students, parents, taxpayers), while at the same time paying attention to the needs of internal customers.

5 Appraisal and Equal Opportunities

When woman manage schools children's academic achievement is greater, teachers have higher morale and parents respond to the school more favourably. These conclusions from American research contrast tellingly with the evidence that in Britain women's promotion prospects for senior management posts have deteriorated in the last 20 years. This evidence of women's leadership abilities contrasts even more dramatically with the common assumption in Britain women's promotion prospects for senior management posts have deteriorated in the last 20 years. This evidence of women's leadership abilities contrasts even more dramatically with the common assumption in Britain that qualities such as detachment and toughness, usually attributed to men, are essential leadership characteristics. The reason for these frequent contrasts between the empirical evidence and our personal assumptions, widely-held social generalizations and some the theoretical hypotheses is that human beings largely act, not on the basis of objective facts or reasonable evidence, but on a series of unexamined assumptions and more or less sophisticated generalisations. Rather than make critical judgments we pre-judge.

We thoughtlessly and habitually use generalizations, including racial and sexual stereotypes, rather than examine each situation afresh. We tend to act emotionally rather than rationally. We condone behaviour in people we like, or who are like us, that we condemn in others. We make scapegoats. We project on to others behavioural characteristics we dislike in ourselves. Admittedly, some people show a greater degree of objectivity, more flexibility to modify their opinions and are less inclined to jump to conclusions than others, but the predisposition remains. Generalizations after all also help us to order and categorize our experience. In appraisal, where teachers are asked to make a series of wide-ranging professional judgements, this psychological and cognitive tendency will be the permanent backcloth.

Early in the debate about the introduction of appraisal for teachers it was argued that an open and formal appraisal scheme would be preferable to the present informal and covert way decisions concerning teachers' careers are made. Inherent in this argument is the assumption that appraisal, by providing a basis of objective criteria and a systematic procedure for professional development and career planning, would counter subjectivity and partiality and contribute to achieving equal opportunities in the widest sense. As the National Steering Group's Report stated, 'appraisal must operate and be seen to operate, fairly and equitably for all teachers' and 'should be used positively to promote equal opportunities by encouraging all teaches to fulfil their potential'. Equal opportunities issues are therefore central to implementing appraisal. Certainly, appraisal will lose credibility with sections of the procession if they perceive structural prejudices and discrimination unaddressed and unaltered.

The under developed level of awareness of equal opportunities issues is one of the many deficiencies in educational management which appraisal tends to highlight. Appraisers need to be aware of their legal responsibilities not to discriminate on grounds of sex, race or marital status and of the danger of stereotyped expectations which result in a biased approach when conducting appraisal. However, exactly how appraisal policies and procedures can address the existing inequalities in processional development and career opportunities for teachers arising from discrimination and stereotyping remains to be considered.

The legislation which outlaws discrimination on the grounds of race, ethnic origins, gender and marital status will apply to appraisal procedures because appraisal contributes to identifying staff development and training needs. Direct or indirect sex discrimination is unlawful under the Sex Discrimination Act 1975 in employment and includes discrimination in opportunities for promotion, transfer, training and education. Direct sex discrimination occurs when a requirement or condition is applied equally to men and women but has the practical effect of disadvantaging a considerably higher proportion of one sex than the other. The 1976 Race Relations Act makes direct or indirect discrimination on the grounds of a person's colour, race, nationality or ethnic origins similarly unlawful.

Therefore, as the NSG Report and the Equal Opportunities Commission recommend, each appraisal scheme should be monitored to assess how it works in practice. This will mean examining the outcomes of the professional targets for development and training identified by appraisal to see if there is an imbalance between sexes or ethnic groups which suggests that unlawful direct or indirect discrimination is occurring. If so, the cause must be identified to ensure that it is not discriminatory. However, the LEA's responsibility does not stop there, for if an employee unlawfully discriminates in the course of employment both employee and employer are responsible whether or not the employer knows or approves of the action, unless the employer has taken reasonable steps to prevent discrimination. Therefore, LEAs must take positive action to prevent appraisers from practising discrimination by, for example, including unbaised managerial practice in the criteria for appraising appraisers and the provision of equal opportunities for all the staff in the criteria for appraising headteachers and by ensuring that nay assessment criteria used in appraisal are not discriminatory. What is also clear is that LEAs must provide appropriate advice on equal opportunities directly to schools and in appraisal training. Knowledge of the legislation alone will not alter the existing management structures and structural prejudices which may cause discrimination and into which appraisal will be incorporated, and the introduction of appraisal requires that these are more fully understood.

Although women outnumber men in the teaching profession they are seriously under-represented in senior positions. In 1685, one in ten male teachers was a headteacher. For women the figure was one in 25. In the secondary sector women formed 55 per cent of the teaching force, but only 31 per cent of those on scale 3 or above, compared to 58 per cent of men. The latest DES returns for the primary sector in England show the same pattern with women disproportionately placed in posts of lower or no responsibility. Women formed 79.9 per cent of the full-time and 87 per cent of the part-time teaching force of these, 76.7 per cent and 96.1 per cent respectively were on scales 1 and 2, compared to 35 per cent of a male full-time teachers. Of the male full-time teachers only 9 per cent had no responsibility, compared to 32 per cent of the women. At the other end of the scale, 32 per cent of men were headteachers and 21 per cent deputy headteachers, compared with 7.5 per cent and 8.5 per cent respectively for women. Furthermore, even these statistics conceal the effect of including nursery and separate infant schools, where almost all teachers are women. In 1987 69.4 per cent of infant/junior headships and 79.6 per cent of junior headships were held by men, although they made up only 25 per cent and 34 per cent of the teachers in such schools.

Men's career chances are therefore substantially better than women's. As the EOC said, this is a wastage of skills and talent and a matter of concern to everyone involved with the teaching profession, because it may indicate a pattern of under-avhievement by women in an area of employment in which there is a well-established traditional of female participation. The causal factors are difficult to identify. An AMMA survey found that although only slightly fewer women described themselves as interested in progressing through the career structure, 57 per cent of men compared to 34 per cent of women were heads, deputy heads or heads of departments. The reason seemed to be that 44 per cent of women teachers, compared with only 14 per cent of men teachers, had a break in service lasting a year or more. Moreover, for men the breaks were usually for further study, training or research - activities which could improve promotion prospects. Women teachers were more likely to have made an enforced sideways move because of a change in the husband's job.

However, there is also extensive evidence that the present situation is in part due to a sex-differentiated management response to women's and men's development needs which determines what type of training and experience is offered to women and men teachers. This is consistent with a survey of the insurance industry where a significant percentage of managers believed women were not interested in a career, while an overwhelming majority of the women considered career advancement a high priority for job satisfaction. In the Civil Service women receive performance ratings as good as men, but lower promotability ratings. Women, it seems, are being excluded from promotion because of under-assessment by their line managers, who may act on unjustified assumptions quite subconsciously and attribute to all women attitudes and opinions which many not he held by the woman being appraised. The existence of such stereotyping is supported by research into women teachers' actual experience of discrimination. Women are commonly questioned in interviews, even by headteachers, on child care arrangements and domestic responsibilities. It is assumed that it is their work which will suffer because women must automatically undertake these responsibilities.

It is obvious that the standard pattern in teaching will be a male manager appraising a female. Even more frequently a white manager will be appraising a black teacher. The danger is that certain assumptions, attitudes and stereotypes which can shape the way an individual's potential is perceived could pervade the appraisal process. It is essential that appraisal training challenges pervade the appraisal process. It is essential that appraisal training challenges rather than reinforces these attitudes. The common sex stereotypes can be categorized neatly. Prestigious qualities such as reason, objectivity, leadership, independence and authority have been attributed to men, while women have been allocated stigmatized qualities such as emotion, irrationality, passivity and dependence. Al-Khalifa argues that recent developments in management theory, which stress school organizational problems as technical problems amenable to rational problem-solving, emphasize characteristics such as 'analytical detachment' and 'hard-nosed roughness' that are commonly seen as 'masculine'. Leadership characteristics are thus seen to correspond to the socially determined masculine sex-role.

Conversely, when women display just these characteristics their ambition and 'hardness' are seen as unnatural and unfeminine and result in pejorative comments. For these are also stereotyped perceptions of the appropriate and inappropriate behaviourr and demeanors of each sex. The common conception of feminity involves modesty, deference, non-aggressiveness and being agreeable. As Spender says, 'In a society which assumes the politeness and deference of women towards men as the norm women who do not defer to men are often judged by men and women as socially unacceptable.' Men may prefer to promote women who are 'passive and non-threatening or at least capable of appearing so'. Cunnison argues that much male humour is designed to undermine women in authority by reminding women of their sexuality and by restating sexual and domestic stereotypes thus implicitly suggesting their administrative incompetence. Women can be deterred from ever assuming posts of responsibility over others and may still be discouraged from promotion by a widely-held assumption that their health and that of their families will suffer. There also remains a deeply-seated belief that men have more right to promotion because they are the main bread-winners.

Women's attitudes also contribute to the generalized supposition that management responsibilities at whatever level are more appropriately undertaken by me. Women are described and sometimes describe themselves as too diffident, poor at job interviews and playing safe in terms of the posts for which they apply. They lack confidence in their competence to teach science because it is perceived as 'masculine' and believe that their male colleagues can compensate for their own limited technical knowledge. Their stereotypes include the perception that male headteavhers will inevitably the authoritarian, unbending and intolerant. Some women teachers also seem to credit men with higher standards and clearer vision, which may affect their ability to contribute professionally to their self-evaluation and to the professional dialogue of appraisal. Unexamined sexual stereotyping in the assumptions of appraisers and in the influence they have on the way women appraises perceive and project themselves and their position can therefore influence appraisal. Appraisers and appraises must be made aware of how sexual stereotyping can be part of our generally shared perceptions and that it can affect self-evaluation and self-presentation.

Male appraisers must be careful to estimate confident, autonomous and assertive women by the same standards as men. Men in general talk more and interrupt more in mixed-sex contexts. Women who consistently and successfully control verbal interaction are frequently criticized by men and are likely to be regarded as 'bitchy', domineering or aggressive. To allow a woman in an appraisal interview 80 per cent of the time to express her views and talk of her priorities may be very difficult for many men. Women may need to learn to state clearly what they want from appraisal and discuss realistic timetables and programmes of action for achieving this because, 'too often women assume that if they have had a good performance review then the manager will automatically put them forward for promotion. In reality this is rarely the case'. Women also tend t get less negative feedback, either through chivalry or a fear the women will burst into tears. Thus they are frequently denied constructive criticism that could improve their performance. Therefore, both men and women need training in giving and receiving feedback constructively.

One stereotype which may particularly influence appraisal is the low status typically ascribed to infant and early years teaching, which is disparaged as an extension of mothering and child care. Other stereotyped assumptions could influence the assessment of classroom management styles. Women teachers who establish discipline through developing relationships and reasoning with pupils rather than dictating to them are taken less seriously than 'hard teachers'.

It should be evident, therefore, that gender stereotypes do need to be considered in appraisal training if appraisal is to be fair and equitable and promote equal opportunities, but it may not be enough. For example, to make allowances for women's diffidence, male appraisers may press on women teachers managerial responsibilities and ambitions which women believe are genuinely inappropriate for them, considering their priorities and values. Men may be usable to appreciate this and misinterpret their reluctance to accept responsibility. This could reinforce the stereotype when what may be involved here are two differing value systems. This possibility is supported by evidence that male and female attitudes to work differ greatly. Comparative studies of men and women in occupations found that most men work for money and career advancement. Men are always looking up the ladder for the main chance whereas women seek job satisfaction, a good working atmosphere and flexibility to fit family life into their careers. The emphasize doing a thorough job and doing the job well. Women work for self-fulfilment, for social relationships and like to feel they are making a contribution and are valued by colleagues. Research suggests that these attitudes are shared by teachers too. Women teachers value classroom teaching and put it as a priority. For them teaching and not management is 'real work'. They are more hesitant about career moves unless they have assessed their readiness. They are more hesitant about factors they feel impinge on their career and professional development, including their classroom strengths and weakness, their commitments outside work, and the obligations these present in maintaining relationships and meeting family needs. In comparison, men teachers show little interest in this kind of self-evaluation, do not mention their home situation and see their future essentially terms of promotion moves.

Many factors aspects of appraisal emphasize contributing to the develoonment of others, whether colleagues or students, and this suggests that male values and modes of behaviours are not the most appropriate models. A value system of responsibilities and care seems more appropriate to appraisal than one of rights and individuality. Also, the American research already quoted indicates that women administrators spend more time with people, care more about individual difference, motivatc more and their staff have more shared professional goals. Women administrators demonstrate a more democratic and participatory management style, exhibit greater knowledge of teaching methods and techniques and create a school climate more condusive to learning. Women also considered 'better listeners' and listening skills are regarded as essential in appraisal. The skill is not only to let the appraisee contribute but to pick up nuances and to detect the underlying assumptions, attitudes and emotions that give the whole picture. It requires both empathy and a concern for others. Men may lack these skills because they are too used to dominating meetings and putting their own arguments. Certainly, women do not believe men are good listeners and often feel that men only take seriously ideas presented by men. In appraisal, listening is given a role as complex as talking, although in social life it is devalued in mixed-sex conversation and associated with passivity. Conventional male styles of verbal interaction will not dominate in appraisal and because this disturbs the balance of power between the sexes may add to the discomfort of interviews with the opposite sex.

In other ways, too, women teachers' values their attitude to being a good teacher and their tendency to be more introspective and hesitant about their professional strengths and weaknesses may be a more appropriate starting point for appraisal. For appraisal is not directly and immediately about promotion, although the qualities and strengths it enhances and develops should not be irrelevant to the qualities and strengths required by teachers with managerial responsibilities. It is about continuous and systematic development as a professional. This makes appraisal relevant for all teachers at whatever stage of their careers. It relates appraisal to improving the equality of learning experiences for children and simultaneously promoting job satisfaction and professional pride and autonomy in teachers. Ironically, male weaknesses, in failing to evaluate the intrinsic quality of job they are doing, in having too much uncritical confidence in their own worth and promotability and in valuing where they are going more than the fulfilment to be gained from making a contribution here and now, may make this essential formative and developmental element of appraisal less satisfying and less convincing for them. There are interesting parallels with boys' and girls' attitudes to records of achievement where there is evidence that girls understand the purpose of the formative process better than boys. The National Steering Committee concluded that girls 'tend to be more forthcoming and skilled in discussion and value the opportunity for one to one contact with their teachers. On the other hand boys tend to have a keener sense of the external audience for the records of achievement rather than relationships.'

However, if by and large men are to be the appraisers then ensuring male commitment to formative appraisal and to the intrinsic and personal elements of professional development must be an essential part of appraisal training. Otherwise male appraisers may find women's attitudes to work deficient because they regard career-centred values as the measure of seriousness and interest in work. If commitment to appraisal of professional development remains superficial and only thinly conceals the expectation that appraisal is about promotion for those with the right qualities - masculine ones - women's likely expectations for appraisal will be severely disappointed. Men in managerial positions could even have their power reinforced. Formative appraisal requires openness and critical self-evaluation, but power, it is argued, often lies with those who do not disclose their vulnerabilities and who abstain from self-revelation and withhold personal information. Remaining aloof while someone else discloses personal information facilitates dominance. If formative appraisal were to reinforce this dominance and leave women more vulnerable, women would have to think carefully about its consequences.

Moreover, if the developmental purpose of appraisal is not fully understood and implemented, the consequences will be dysfunctional. Appraisal would not then contribute to improving professional dialogue or to a better understanding and appreciation of the skills of teaching or to sharing what we learn to improve the teaching and learning environment of the school. It would not help teachers fulfil their potential. Appraisal as conceived by the pilot projects and the NSG, however, will focus on reflection, self-evaluation, professional development and improving teaching and learning; and not only on promotion. It is likely to change the focus of teaching to one that is more congenial to women. As managerial responsibilities begin to include responsibility for appraisal - and thus the responsibility to encourage the skills of teaching analysis and classroom observation and obligations to the development of professional colleagues - managerial roles will also be more in line with women's values. The role of headteacher as an educational leader will be more attractive to women than the role of headteacher as administrator.

The under-presentation of teachers from ethnic minority groups is other major concern to all those in education and from January 1990 returns must be made on the ethnic origins of teachers. The aim is to provide data to support fair and equal employment opportunities and additional details of sex, age, phase, specialism and form of employment will be collected by the DES. However, in 1988 a survey of eight LEAs found that only two per cent of teachers was black and evidence showed that they were disproportionately on the lower salary scales. It concluded that teachers from ethnic minorities do not enjoy the same career progression as white teachers and headteachers do not encourage them to apply for vacancies within the school in the same way as white teachers. An ILEA survey in 1987 found that 'black teachers were severely and negatively affected during reorganization and amalgamations of schools when demotions were more likely for black teachers than promotions or holding on to their substantive posts.'

In order to counteract structural prejudices and discrimination, appraisal training will similarly nerd to acknowledge the context in which ethnic minority teachers find themselves - a context which is rarely openly discussed. Teachers from ethnic minorities will be well aware of racial prejudice and stereotypes, of racial attracts on minority groups and of racist graffiti. These teachers may even have experienced racist remarks from their own teachers and racist attitudes restricting their own educational achievement by an underestimate of their potential. Grievances on grounds of racial harassment are not unknown in teaching, although there is little firm evidence of their extent. There is also the 'insidious, unconscious racism of white teachers who fail to recognize that their black colleagues may feel ill at ease in a mainly white staff room or may need some support to cope with harassment they suffer outside school'. However, this social context and the way it influences relationships with colleagues and their perceptions is not always understood in teaching.

Only Now are black teachers' experience and perspectives of schools and their management finding a wider audience. These experiences include having identity, as black persons and members of minority groups, ignored, particularly as students, yet finding their working lives dominated by issues to do with race. Assumptions are made that black teachers can speak for all the local black community even if they personally know little about other ethnic groups and cultures.

A revealing example of this pervasive attitude occurs in a supposedly exemplary appraisal interview. A young teacher is asked, 'Have there been any disappointments during the year?' and responds with, 'Not really apart from the fact that I still don't have my own class. I think that people see me as some sort of superior classroom helper. I'm a fully qualified teacher, but just because I can speak Punjabi I have to stay....The explanatory comment acknowledges this is an important and valid point and a highly emotional issue which a teacher would quite legitimately want to make highly emotional issue which a teacher would quite legitimately want to make sure was raised during the appraisal interview. The advice to the appraiser is that one cannot allow the interview to be side-tracked from the agreed agenda because the headteacher has to deploy the staff to meet the children's needs. Thus the issues of equal opportunities, structural prejudice and personal identity are ignored.

Teachers from ethnic minorities have the same right to opportunities for complete professional development from appraisal and the same right to be regarded as individuals, which means that their specific needs and experience as a part of a minority group cannot be ignored. School management must become aware of how it may be involving these reachers unreasonably. Fair and equal treatment means varying and sensitive treatment. It requires understanding, confidence and maturity in the appraiser which may not be acquired unless the introductory materials and appraisal training emphasize the significance of these issues and help appraisers to develop the necessary understanding and skills.

It is perhaps only now being recognized that prejudices that limit equality of opportunity extend to stereotyped assumptions about what is appropriate and beneficial at varying ages. Potentially this is sexual discrimination and the EOC recommends that on these grounds age limits for access to training and promotion should questioned. However, on all grounds for equality, appraisal training should ensure that it is not assumed that in-service training (with its related expenses) is inappropriate for those near retirement or that teachers over 50 will prefer premature retirement to challenges in the classroom and increased responsibilities. In fact, the AMMA survey found 70 per cent of the 40-49 age group and 48 per cent of the over -50s still interested in progressing in their career.

There are also important factors which are relevant to inter-personal skills training. Although individuals vary, it is generally more difficult to adapt one's teaching styles if these are the product of some 30 years' experience. all change brings with it a sense of becoming de-skilled and demoralized and a certain percentage of fear. Appraisers should be particularly careful not to damage the sense of self-worth and the lifetime achievement of those very near the end of their teaching career and to allow for the psychological process of adapting to retirement. Appraisal by younger teachers may threaten the sense of dignity of older teachers. Mores, courtesies and vocabularies do change but nothing in appraisal should precipitate the decision of an experienced but perhaps demoralized professional to leave teaching. Many teachers, particularly men, who tend to have greater expectations of promotion, must come to terms with disappointment as they age. Sometimes male anger and resentment may be deflected on to women, especially those on their way up. As appraisers, women may have to learn to manage this and turn it into something positive. Certainly, to archive the trust and confidence of these experienced classroom teachers will require considerable professional an personal skills.

It should now be obvious that issues of equal opportunities must be integrated at every stage of implementing appraisal. LEAs have been asked to set the climate for appraisal and to raise awareness.

In particular, positive reassurances should be given at this stage that equal opportunities will be respected. Each LEA should make it clear that the existence of racial and sexual harassment is a legitimate area of concern. Sexual harassment is possibly the most difficult area of inter-personal relationships in appraisal. It has been defined by the NUT as 'any uninvited, unreciprocated and unwelcome physical contact, comment, suggestion, joke or attention which is offensive to the person involved and causes that person to feel threatened, humiliated, patronised or embarrassed.' It may create a threatening and intimidating working environment, adversely affect job performance and, in extreme cases, may cause a person to seek to leave the school. Sexual harassment is widespread with surveys all showing a high proportion of women reporting unwanted attentions from men.

In the only specific survey of women secondary teachers 65 per cent of the 246 respondents had experienced sexual harassment, predominantly from male colleagues. The most common experience, of being eyes up and down or of suggestive looks at parts of the body, was recorded by two in five of the respondents. Regular sexual jokes and innuendo were reported almost as often. More than one in five of the women teachers had experienced 'touching, brushing against, patting, pincing or grabbing.' Even more seriously one in ten reported a direct sexual proposition and six reported forcible sexual aggression from male colleagues. For appraisal, the most serious aspect is likely to be the pervasiveness of suggestive looks and sexual innuendo. Classroom observation could become a degrading and humiliating experience for women teachers, resulting in considerable modifications to manner, behaviour and dress, and imposing a high degree of unnaturalness in order to avoid being the object of unwanted sexual attention in a professional teaching environment. women will be unable to continue the avoidance tactics reported by a third of the respondents into survey. Sexual remarks, jokes and innuendo can be part of 'staff room banter' and to complain can be regarded as churlish. Like black people complaining of racism, women are often told that they are imagining that actions are suggestive or lascivious. Yet sexual jokes and generally making fun of women constantly draw attention back to a woman's sex and feminity. Subtly, this implies that women are less competent and less committed to their job and undermines their authority.

If appraisal is to be as positive for women as for men these issues will have to be confronted to end what one teacher is the survey described a s 'fighting two battles - the things you want to achieve professionally and how to cope with men, because in their eyes you are a woman and not a teacher.' Women teachers must feel confident that they will not have to tolerate the danger of behaviour which may be bearable in the semi-social context of the staffroom but which impairs and diminishes the professional interaction essential in appraisal. It would also be unendurable for women teachers who have experienced 'touching up' were the appraiser the perpetrator. Close proximity in a private interviewing room would bring the fear of humiliation and negate a woman teacher's ability to evaluate her professional contribution. However, sexual harassment is often unreported because it causes high levels of anxiety and stress. Women find it difficult to talk about. In the Birmingham survey 74 per cent of the women did not complain at all, largely because they believed the reaction would be negative and that what had happened would not be regarded as serious enough; when they did complain 31 per cent reported that no action was taken and where action was taken 71 percent was not satisfied with the outcome.

Appraisal requires an open recognition that sexual harassment is properly regarded as a disciplinary misdemeanor which will tangibly affect career prospects if a managerial position is exploited. LEAs must take particular care to deal effectively with all complaints of harassment and, most importantly, not assume that they are made by women who are over sensitive. Awareness-rising materials, training courses for appraisers, and

management courses should raise the issue so that before the introduction of appraisal each school examines whether its ethos and climate allows all its teachers the same personal respect. It should be widely acknowledged during awareness raising that the selection of an appraiser would be reconsidered sonsitively if sexual or racial harassment was a factor.

Satisfactory appraisal should also include an assessment of the awareness of equal opportunities issues within the LEA. The legal basis for direct and indirect discrimination and the NSG recommendation on the dangers of stereotyping and bias should be widely disseminated and referred to in both the preliminary literature and the training progrmmes. The training programme should incorporate the factual information on the position of women and ethnic minority teachers in the profession and disseminate relevant research. Some authorities may wish to disseminate their own equal opportunities policies and some schools may consider integrating gender and race issues raised by appraisal with issues related to the curriculum and in line with their own school policies. A balance here between age, sex, ethnic grouping and position in the teaching hierarchy can do a great deal to overcome the imbalance in a typical school's management structure and contribute to creating the right climate for emphasizing equal opportunities in appraisal.

The principle that appraisers must guard against any thing that distorts reality, favourably or unfavourably, is embodied in all appraisal schemes and so sexual and racial stereotypes, and the unexamined prejudices and assumptions which are often part of our behaviour patterns must be considered and explained in appraisal training. For example, performance or behaviour which would be overlooked or condoned in one sex must not be noted as significant in the other. Appraises, too, need to understand the significance of stereotyping in their inter-personal transactions and in self-evaluation and self-presentation. Undoubtedly this will be one of the more difficult areas of training since it requires not only attitudinal changes but the development of self-critical skills. The training must be experimental and allow teachers the chance to recognize when they are using unexamined assumptions and stereotypes. Video-taped situations and paired observation can help to alert teachers to what not to do. In skills such as handling potential conflict it is likely that repeated practice, coaching and remedial training will be appropriate. For some people this aspect of appraisal training will not be comfortable and schools and LEAs should give serious consideration to the need for counseling both during training and to protect those who feel unfairly treated because of intended or unintended stereotyping when appraisal is implemented.

Equal opportunities should also be part of the criteria for assessing the school and the educational system. The extent to which the LEA or the school is delivering equal opportunities can be measured by the nature of the staffing structure, the allocation of incentive allowances and the outcomes of appraisal. To be effective, this requires efficient monitoring of where both ethnic minority group teachers and women teachers are in the educational system relative to their experience and qualifications.

LEAs will also have to consider how well their own structures reflect a concern for equal opportunities issues. Men make up 75.5 per cent of the total advisors but women make up 40 per cent of the primary advisers and only 17.5 per cent of the secondary ones. It is likely that similar sexual and racial stereotypes and similar prejudices are prevalent with in LEA management. The need to update and enhance the skills of LEA advisers and officers is now widely recognized and should include equal opportunities issues, particularly in the light of the introduction of appraisal. Researchers, too, can contribute by always looking for possible differences in male and female teachers' experiences, skills and attitudes in teaching. Age and membership of an ethnic minority group should be regarded as possibly significant variables wherever relevant. In this way we can improve the evidential base, against which we can test our assumptions.

However, all this will be irrelevant if sensititive and practical steps are not taken genuinely to face gender and race issues in schools. Situations where graffiti is referred to in assembly because of the damage to property rather than for its racist nature and where sexual harassment by students is regarded as a disciplinary failure in the teacher rather than an issue for the school, cannot coexist with a climate that ensures a fair appraisal for all teachers. Neither can we ignore the influence practical problems such a lack of child care facilities have on women's ability to concentrate on their own professional development through INSET. The approach to equal opportunities must be consistent and unvarying or else the intent that appraisal should be used positively to promote equal opportunities will lose its credibility.

It is difficult to see how writers on appraisal can describe it as a fairer and more up-to-date basis for making professional judgments and yet, as so many do, ignore equal opportunities issues entirely. The NSG has quite properly placed for a and equitable treatment of all teachers at the centre of the appraisal process and has stated categorically that appraisal should be used positively *to promote equal opportunities* by encouraging all teachers to fulfil their potential. It has recognized that stereotyping and the bias that arises from both prejudice and partiality are barriers to fairness and equity. The starkfact is that we can make no attempt at an objective assessment without consciously and explicitly considering the effect our unexamined assumptions and our own value system have on the process and without testing our assumptions against behavioural and other evidence. the applies in every appraisal. The issues raised by gender, race and age are, however, deeply embedded in both our subconscious and our emotive ways of thinking. They must be faced directly and specifically. The introduction of appraisal moves equal opportunities issues to the pivotal point in awareness raising and training and makes this the greatest challenge and the greatest opportunity for radical change in the structure and the values of the teaching profession.

6 Student Satisfaction and Perceptions of Quality

Perceptions and expectations of quality

The quality debate in higher education traditionally focuses on whether profit-orientated private sector concepts can be readily transferred to the public sector. This is a complex issue but even the limited view of the student, as a customer or client, goes against the grain of many in HE. They are very reluctant to empower a group who are traditionally treated as passive recipients of education.

Both the broad consumer perspective, that service quality can be equated to the extent to which the perceived level of service delivered matches consumer expectations and the more specific view that service satisfaction equals consumer perception minus consumer expectation, is not without problems in the HE context. However, the implication that satisfaction will result if perceptions are greater than expectations has a great deal of intuitive appeal.

This balance between consumers' perceptions and expectations as a measure of service quality has been fairly widely-discussed and appears to be useful. Nevertheless antagonists to the quality initiative often argue that in the HE context it is futile to attempt to define quality in this way because student expectations are poorly developed, variable and unpredictable. Validly measuring student perceptions and expectations is not a simple matter but can be approached in a systematic way to reveal useful information.

to complicate matters further, antagonists to the quality initiative often point out that different stakeholders in HE will all have different sorts of expectations from a particular institution or service. Consequently they claim that different stakeholders will have disparate ideas about :"quality". jeopardising any attempt at valid assessment. Clearly there is more than one client group to be considered in examining the perceived value of higher education, but this does not mean that these various perceptions cannot be systematically studied.

Despite these conceptual caveats, two things are clear. First, the most important client group are the "front-line" consumers, the students themselves. Second, and equally important, it is evident that "quality" will become the principal means by which higher education institutes will attempt to differentiate themselves from their educational competitors.

The work of the SSRU

Unit recently, students' views of their academic experience had been of interest only to a handful of educational evaluators but increasingly the value of this information has been recognised. The realisation that students' attitudes and perceptions are not only interesting that may play a central role in shaping the decisions of those who manage our higher education institutes has widespread implications.

Since its inception in 1988, the Student Satisfaction Research Unit (SSRU) at Birnningham Polytechnic has produced an abundance of information related to student perceptions of educational quality and their satisfaction with their educational experience. Our interest in quality and their satisfaction with their educational experience. Our interest in quality and our attempts to measure it through student satisfaction have three broad aims. First, we are attempting to identify and examine the components of satisfaction and the components of quality and to consider how these two domains are interrelated. Second, we are investigating whether there is a common core to students' perceptions of satisfaction and quality. third, we are attempting to model student satisfaction and quality of education and to represent this model in ways which are designed to inform management decision and policy-making.

Nowadays, collecting information about student satisfaction in educational establishments is a growth industry. Information of this kind has the potential benefit of guiding management decision-making with respect to the planning and provision of educational services. Those HE managers who can clearly identify and subsequently measure client-centered quality will be able to capitalise on student-based information to support their claims for resources.

Eliciting areas of student concern

One approach to directly eliciting students' views of the Polytechnic which has proved to be particularly productive over the last few years is a form of Nominal Group Technique which we have dubbed the "Group Feedback Strategy" (GFS). Essentially this takes the form of a structured participative discussion with groups of students in order to provoke a span of student nominated indicators of satisfaction and dissatisfaction.Experience has shown that engendering an atmosphere of frank and open communication encourages students to talk freely and honestly about what their education means to them. These sessions, facilitated by experienced group leaders, generally result in eliciting a wide and diverse range of satisfiers and dissatisfiers which are used on an annual basis to update the design of the instruments used to student satisfaction in Polytechnic. The GFS exercise is used primarily as a device to validate the content of the questionnaire survey prior to it's annual administration, although the procedure itself produces some interesting findings. Some results of the GFS session are described in the next section.

Three factors were used to define the sample frame:

a Faculty - 8 categories in all (health and Social Sciences, Built environment etc.)

b PFC Classification - 3 categories (Postgraduate, Degree and Other)

c Mode of Attendance - 3 categories (Full-time, Part-time and Sandwich).

16 classes were representatively sampled from this frame and participated in GFS exercises, enabling the views of 265 students to be obtained.

It is worth noting that the overwhelming majority of students welcomed the opportunity to express their opinions in a confidential climate and were delighted to have some input into any future decision-making process.

Areas of student satisfaction and dissatisfaction

The outcomes of the GFS procedure were consensus, but wide-ranging, lists of satisfiers and dissatisfiers elicited from students in each of the 16 participating classes. In order to provide a framework for analysing these unstructured statements, each "good" or "bad" statement was allocated to one or more of 44 core activities which had been identified through synthesising categories used in our previous work. these core activities are reasonably exhaustive of students' concerns and are clearly associated with student satisfaction and dissatisfaction. The 44 core activities themselves represent four broad areas of student concern. the four broad areas are shown in Table together with a mean percentage satisfaction score for each area (derived from the relative proportion of good and bad statements allocated to each area).

1.	Teaching/Learning Activity Area	36.9%
2.	Personal/Interpersonal Activity Area	76.5%
3.	Using Facilities Activity Area	17.6%
4.	Spending/ Budgeting Activity Area	4.6%

Areas of student concern

These results are interesting because they suggest that students have a natural tendency to regard some aspects of their educational experience as innately and potentially more satisfying than others. The Personal and Interpersonal area which includes such activities as "broadening my experience and outlook". "socialising with other students" and "talking to staff freely and openly" is seen in a very positive light (77%) whereas Spending and Budgeting has little potential for satisfaction (5%). Teaching and Learning Activities can provide some satisfaction (37%) whereas Using Facilities generally tends to be a focus for discontent (18%). In other words students tend to stress negative aspects or grievances when considering their finances or using polytechnic facilities. IN contrast, students are inclined to be more positive when considering their study experiences and even more enthusiastic when reflecting on their personal and interpersonal experiences.

Ratings of importance

In addition to expressing their opinions about their likes and dislikes, students were also required to each of the 44 core activities with respect to 5two aspects of importance. The first rating was of the importance of each activity to enhancing the effectiveness of study; the second rating was of the importance of each activity to enhancing students' personal sense of well-being. Part of our purpose was to investigate the relationship between these twin aspects of importance in order to provide information about students' priorities.

The results revealed that students see some activities as consistently more important than others. some activities were seen as critical to both study effectiveness and personal well-being. Some other activities were perceived as relatively unimportant in both domains; yet others were seen as differentially important to effectiveness of study or well-being. the two ratings of importance appeared to be tapping different underlying student perceptions. Table below shows the five most and the five least important activities together with their associated correlations between ratings of importance to effective study and importance to personal well-being.

Most important Activities for Effective Study	Rank
Understanding the content of lectures	1 0.30
Receiving well organised and structured tuition	2 0.24
Receiving feedback on assess work	3 0.40
Receiving guidance and supervision by staff	4 0.41
Using time productively	5 0.45
Most Important Activities for Enhancing Well-Being	
Paying my way/spending/budgeting	1 0.69
Increasing my self confidence	2 0.67
Having a base to leave personal property	3 0.59
Receiving well organised and structured tuition	4 0.24
Receiving feedback on assessed work	5= 0.60
Broadening my experience and outlook	5= 0.40
Least Important Activities for Effective Study	
Joining societies and groups	1 0.66
Using the accommodation service	2 0.77
Using student services (e.g. medical etc)	3 0.80
Using canteen facilities	4 0.59
Buying acceptable (cost, range & quality) food...	5 0.60
Least Important Activities for Enhancing Well-Being	
Using the accommodation service	1 0.77
Joining societies and groups	2 0.66
Accessing relevant information form Faculty learning Centres	3= 0.64
Using student services (e.g. medial etc	3= 0.80
Using Faculty Learning Centres	5= 0.65
Accessing relevant information from IT facilities	5= 0.66

Table Most important and least important activities.

Mapping satisfaction and importance ratings

Both satisfaction and importance are essential ways of considering students' perceptions of their educational activities. Polcyn has suggested that importance and satisfaction can be represented as quadrants on a graph and each quadrant has different organisational implications.

The graph shows that both the Spending/Budgeting Area and the Teaching/Learning Area fall within Quadrant A. consequently, both areas may be regarded as those where management may consider intervention a priority. Spending and budgeting is an area of increasing concern to students at Polytechnics and this is reflected in its position on the graph. Personal and Interpersonal Concerns fall within Quadrant B on the graph and this reflects students repeatedly-voiced opinion that being able to approach teaching staff and relate to them in a free and open manner is of great importance to their general levels of satisfaction. From the management perspective, the graph shows that it is necessary to maintain course organisation so that opportunities for good quality interaction between staff and students are optimised. Using Facilities can be seen to be the least important of the four broad areas and it can be seen to fall in Quadrant C. Often it seems that good student facilities are weighted as more critical by management than they are by students themselves. The graph shows that no area falls within quadrant D and this is probably an outcome of the GFS procedure itself which is designed to target issues of high importance rather than focus on issues of little or no importance.

7 Strategies for Management Development: Towards Coherence?

At the outset it might be helpful to define our understanding of 'management' and therefore refer the reader to two existing definitions of the word. Both are task-focused and point to the central role of the people, the human resources, in an institution to achieve the tasks. So 'management' is 'the process of securing decisions about what activities the organisation will undertake, and mobilising the human and material resources to undertake them'; or it is, 'achieving goals by, with and through people and managers and all those responsible for the world of other adults'. In this context 'management development' can be defined as, 'the process whereby the management function of an organisation is performed with increasing effectiveness'.

There s clearly an imperative to improve strategies for management development at all levels in the education service. For example, Her Majesty's Inspectors reporting on school and college inspections during the period 1982/86 wrote that, 'one of the most significant determinants of a good school was high-quality leadership and good management'. This was followed by a statement from the Senior Chief Inspector reporting on the state of England's education service and quoted in the *Times Educational Supplement* in 1990. He said,'...the management of schools leaves much to be desired. In only about a third of those inspected was senior management judged to be particularly effective'.[...] Therefore, the need for more coherent and effective strategies for school management development has never been more urgent.

Strategic planning for management development

The effective delivery of management development must begin with strategic planning at several levels in the education service.

Schools There is now much good practice available in terms of the effective planning and delivery of staff development, and within this broader context for management development, at school level. Such good practice must now become normal practice in all schools. The planning should have three main strands. The first is the drawing up of an institutional development plan (IDP) which is informed by an evaluation of the school. The IDP, a relatively brief and readable document, will then be available as a basis for all other aspects of school planning such as curriculum development, staffing, budgeting and making decisions about the priorities for staff development.

The second is the establishment of a staff development committee which is broadly representative of all groups on the staff and has appropriate delegated authority to plan and deliver a school's programme of staff in-service education and training within the agreed framework of priorities set out in the IDP.

The third is a scheme of staff appraisal which is adequately resource and provides information about individual development needs. Suitably anonymized, the outcomes of staff appraisal should be used as an additional source of background information by the staff development committee as they plan the use of the resources allocated to them.

Local network Local networks can help to prevent school-focused staff development from becoming too inward-looking by providing opportunities to work with colleagues fro, other schools in the area.

Regional and national Effective planning for management development also requires a broader perspective at regional and national levels to help avoid too much 're-invention of wheels' and also to address strategic issues of more than local importance like the accreditation of programmes of management development and the preparation for headship.

Other agencies Several other agencies will continue to make a significant contribution to management development at all levels,

(1) *Industry*: One of the most encouraging features of school management development over the past few years has been the increased involvement of personnel from industry working on the basis of a partnership with education. A less regular feature of such co-operative arrangements in the movement of personnel *from* industry *into* schools or other aspects of the education service.

(2) *Professional associations*: The teacher associations have also shown an increasing

commitment to the professional development of their members and many now offer a wide range of courses and other forms of in-service education and training.

(3) *Higher education and independent providers*: Higher education and a growing number o independent providers will continue to contribute to school management development at all levels. IN the future their success or failure in this role will depend much more on the pressures of the marketplace, Schools, consortia and other networks of institutions or individuals will be shopping around for the best and most appropriate opportunities for management development at prices which they can afford.

Succession planning and career development

An overall strategy for management development should embrace the maintenance and development of institutional management structures as well as the personal development of individual managers. From time to time key people will leave an institution for a variety of reasons and, although man individual resignations are unpredictable, local a regional patterns in vacancies are discernible. Succession planning begins with this type of analysis and uses the results to consider the action required to increase the chances of filling vacancies with a minimum loss of overall management performance in an organization.

Large organizations are more able to implement in house systems of succession planning and can fill many vacancies through internal promotion. Schools on the other hand are preventative of small and medium-sized organizations which can do much less to predict succession problems and must usually resort to external appointments to fill their vacancies. This means that they are more vulnerable to market forces over which they have little control. There is a danger that the move towards the local management of schools will compound the problem of fragmentation in the education service and put further limits on the possibility of succession planning at local level.

However, the education service as a whole has usually 'grown; its own managers. It is therefore quite possible to envisage on approach to succession planning which has a local perspective provided that overall data about teacher supply and conditions is available at national level. Such data could then be supplemented by regional and local knowledge of staffing structures in schools, age structures, wastage rates and recruitment patterns which are potentially available to local education authorities. Armed with this knowledge, LEA s and consortia of schools would then be in a position to adopt a more positive approach to succession planning. For example, they could take steps to increase the number of qualified application for particular types of vacancy in the locality by joint advertising, training and development programmes. Both the development and the selection of staff could be informed, particularly at senior level, by the use of regional educational assessment centres which would provide a profile of managerial potential.

Individual career development is clearly an important concomitant of succession planning. In school staff development and the wider provision of inservice education and training must find the right balance between the requirements of the present job, personal professional growth and preparation for promotion. Certainly careers advice and appropriate support in the planning of a personal development programme should be available to all teachers as should opportunities to gain experience of management responsibilities at a higher level.

Ideally such advice and support will be seen as essential features of staff appraisal schemes and staff development committees. Special attention is needed for those whose career patterns have been interrupted.

Assessment for management development

Withcut some assessment of need, the time and money spent on the management development of an individual can be wasted or, at least, be of only limited value. Staff appraisal and self-analysis questionnaires may help to inform development needs but both are relatively limited and blunt instruments. There would be greater coherence at all levels of management development if we could approach the assessment of need, and then the provision of development, using a micro-surgeon's knife rather than the traditional blunderbuss, firing off development opportunities in the hope that a few will strike individual targets.

There is also much to be gained by raising the profile of personal and generic management competencies as a vital component of development programmes alongside the more traditional tasks-related and job-specific aspects of middle and senior management roles in schools.

For example, there are plenty of courses available to learn about curriculum planning, timetabling, budgeting and marketing the school but far fewer opportunities which focus on the development of generic competencies like judgement, decisiveness, leadership and written communication.

The Educational Assessment Centre project, started in September 1990 and based in Oxford, worked with 28 clients from the maintained and independent school sectors in England, Wales and Scotland. It is an important and ambitious attempt to meet both the requirements outlined above by providing senior staff with a detailed diagnostic profile for further professional development based on 12 generic management competencies. The initial aim of the EAC project is to improved the management competencies of further headteachers so that they will be effective managers as well as successful educators. It should be emphasized that the project is applicable to management development in all aspects and phases of the education service.

Assessment centres have been used in both the public and private sectors of employment for over 50 years to inform the process of developing and selecting senior managers. Their use has been restricted to senior levels primarily because assessment centres that productive valid and reliable data are relatively expensive to establish and operate.

Establishing an assessment centre in particular occupational setting is a complex and technical process which draws on the expertise psychologists and professionals. The EAC model being adapted for use in the UK has been in operation for about 15 years in North America and Australia. It has been the subject of two large scale independent research studies and its high quality has now been proven.

There are four key stages in the establishment of any assessment centre and they have been followed in setting up the EAC project:

Identifying the management competencies required for success

In the case of the EAC this would refer to success as a head. It will be reviewed and modified in the light of the experience gained from the pilot phase of the EAC project.

Designing job-related exercises to test the competencies

Research suggests that the performance of participants on job-related exercises does provide good evidence of their likely behaviour on the actual job.

At the heart of a high-quality assessment centre is the successful design of the job-related exercises to simulate a particular job and to tease out the management competencies.

Training assessors to assess the performance of participants on the job-related exercises.

Reflection over many years on the use of assessment centres suggests that they are most effective when the assessors are doing, or have done, the job for which the centre has been designed to assess potential. Therefore the assessors at the EAC are in most cases heads, those with headship experience or senior education officers/advisors who regularly work with senior teams in schools. The assessors undertake a rigorous and demanding training course and thee is a small failure rate. Not all those in senior positions within the education service have the particular skills required to be an effective assessor.

Producing a personal report about each EAC participant

It is important to stress that an EAC is a *process* not a place. However the participants and assessors will obviously assemble at a particular place, usually a hotel or management centre, to go through the process. It takes about one and a half days for the participants to complete the exercises observed by the assessors. At this point the participants depart and the assessors then spend a further two to three days in 'consensus'. They go through every aspect of each participant's performance on the exercises in fine detail and agree the performance ratings. Each participant will have been directly observed by five of the assessor team during the completion of the exercises so that there is a broadly based, and therefore more objective, overview of performance. At the end of consensus each assessor will write a final report on one participant but will draw on the views of the whole assessor team. The report is structured according to the 12 management competencies with a section of strengths followed by a section of competencies which need improvement and finally some suggestions for further professional development. Within 15 working days of the ends of an EAC each participants returns for a feedback interview with the director when they receive their personal copy of the report.

Educational Assessment Centre: the relationship between the twelve competencies and the job-related exercises

Management competencies Leaderless group discussions Fact-finding In-trays Interview

1. Problem analysis
2. Judgement
3. Organizational ability
4. Decisiveness
5. Leadership
6. Sensitivity
7. Stress tolerance
8. Oral communication
9. Written communication
10. Range of interest
11. Personal motivation
12. Educational values

Early experience of the first EACs in the UK is confirming the fact that they have enormous potential to inform professional development by providing a diagnostic profile of strengths and weaknesses across 12 vital management competencies.

The initial focus for further development is always on the things that a participant can do 'on the job' supplemented by the opportunity to spend some time alongside another senior colleague in a nearby school. This can provide the opportunity to observe someone with a difference style working in a less familiar context. For a deputy head wanting to prepare for headship, this might mean working more regularly with their own head (acting as a 'coach') and spending time alongside another experienced head. To help with this developmental support, the EAC project is providing training for experienced heads in the process-skills of coaching and monitoring.

A portfolio of further professional development opportunities is also being prepared. This will include a range of high quality and cost-effective opportunities currently available from providers of management development in both the private and public sectors. They have been analysed according to the 12 competencies so that if, for example, a participant is relatively weak in problem analysis, judgement, organizational ability and leadership then he can be directed to appropriate management development which focuses on that particular cluster of competencies. In so doing, we believe that the EAC process is getting us closer to the 'micro-surgeon's knife' of professional development referred to earlier in the section.

It is expected that EAC participants will also draw on other forms of support for their further development like the LEA, higher education, industrial placements and professional associations. Inevitably the EAC process will lead some participants away from headship as the next career move and towards alternatives which would better utilize their particular range of strengths. This outcome of the EAC process is just as important as the further development of those who will move on to headship in improving the quality of the next generation of heads. Being promoted to one's 'level of incompetence' is potentially disastrous for both the individual and the institution, particularly if that level is headship.

Although the main thrust of the EAC project is towards the *development* of further heads, the process can also be adapted to help inform the selection procedure for headship. A quite separate selection package has been trailed and will be made available to school governing bodies to use as part of the appointment procedure. It is hoped that this source of more objective data will be used widely by governing bodies in the future to guide their decisions when appointing a new head. The aim is certainly not to produce a clone of some ideal 'management-man' or 'woman' as heads of the future, but to acknowledge that heads do need a reasonably strong profile of management competencies (as well as other qualities) if they are to be really effective and run good schools.

Both the developmental and selection uses of the EAC process will enhance succession planning and career development at senior levels.

They should also help to achieve a much needed cultural shift to the way in which the teaching profession (and we are not along in this) approaches the assessment of performance. We are too often stuck in the fruit of seeing each other through rose-coloured glasses. For example, applicants for promotion are regarded as suspect if their references are not full of superlatives and yet, realizing that nobody can be that perfect, appointment panels are then reduced to frantically reading between the lines of a reference to search for the chinks in the shining armour or to making furtive phone-calls to current employers for an 'off the record' honest assessment.

Staff appraisal more often than not ends up with a general pat on the back with inadequate evidence about performance. Few line-managers get proper training in the skills of appraisal interviewing or how to give positive criticism to a colleague. Therefore who can blame them if they back off the more demanding aspects of an appraisal interview when it gets to the discussion about areas of relative weakness followed by the planning of a programme of further development?

The EAC process provides the detailed evidence on which judgements about an important aspect of performance (management competency) may be based. It is also much more open and honest than traditional methods for the assessment of performance. EAC participants are therefore at the cutting edge of an important cultural shift. Bearing this reality in mind, it is reassuring for the participants that the EAC process takes place on 'neutral territory' well away from their own school or employing authority.

Great care is taken to ensure that the assessors at a particular EAC are not known personally or professionally to any of the participants and that the security of the final report is carefully safeguarded.

The EAC assessors are also at the cutting edge of new attitudes to the assessment of performance. Remember that they are senior staff, usually heads, who agree to undertake assessor training, which they could fail, and also to put themselves in a learning situation alongside a group of their peers. The need [is] for heads to become 'head-learners', if they are to lead by example and encourage both staff and pupils in the view that education is a life-long experience.

Although the full EAC process may be too expensive for use outside the development and selection of heads, the principles and procedures on which it is based could be adapted for much wider use throughout education in assessment for management development.

Preparation for leadership

Leadership now and in the future

At the Educational Assessment Centre 'leadership' is one of the 12 management compentencies. It is quite narrowly defined as 'the ability to get others involved in solving problems; the ability to recognize when a group requires direction, to interact with a group effectively and to guide them to the accomplishment of a task'. A similar task-oriented definition is provided by Hughes *et al* although they expand it slightly to include an external aspect of the role: 'Professional leadership is concerned with task achievement, with group maintenance and development, and with the external, representative aspects of the role'.

Leadership skills at this level are not innate but can be acquired and developed. For example, Adair says, 'The traditional or "qualities" approach to leadership suggests that the person who emerges as a leader in a group does so because he possesses certain traits. This view has been rejected by academics.'

Both the above definitions of leadership make explicit the fact that leaders should not make all the decisions or carry out all the tasks in an organization themselves. Rather they should have the skill to empower and guide others in the accomplishment of tasks. The skills required to do this will focus on team-building. However such definitions mark a radical shift away from the autocratic model of management.

Hughes' description of the two main sub-roles of headship-leading professional and chief executive—presents a composite image of institutional leadership. The two sub-roles are, in practice, closely inter-related and must be maintained in a creative, not a destructive, tension. Hughes in an earlier publication puts it this way:

The innovating head, it appears, relies partly on exerting influence on staff colleagues as a fellow professional : equally, however, he accepts his position as chief executive, and uses the organizational controls which are available to him to get things moving. Professional and executive considerations reinforce each other as complementary aspects of a coherent and unified strategy.

The framework of qualities which holds these two sub-roles together in a 'coherent and unified strategy' and infuses all aspects of leadership is the individual's values, attitudes and vision. The Biblical adage, 'without vision the people perish' has taken on a new meaning as a growing body of research has demonstrated that the most successful organizations have leaders with a strong personal commitment to a particular set of values plus a clear vision for the future. This is probably what commentators are referring to when they speak of the 'charismatic' aspects of leadership. Successful leaders will have a vision which inspires the commitment of other people.

It should be noted that all the boundaries are dotted lines indicating that the two leadership sub-roles continually interact with each other, that both sub-roles are influenced by an individual's values.

attitudes and vision and that effective leaders are willing to modify their position result of new demands and changing influences from outside.

Coherence in the preparation for leadership

The role of the head is rarely well-defined, certainly not in official documents. Hall *et al*, having conducted research on headteachers at work, concluded:

Our description and discussion of how secondary school headship is performed have recorded how different individual role interpretations can be. This degree of variance raises the question of whether government ... should set out some guidelines for school management.

However, it may be better that more detailed guidelines have not been set out centrally because they would almost inevitably become ossified and inhibit the redefinition that would be necessary as the context of schools changes. This is also one of the main argument against a national staff college for training heads

Nevertheless, we do need some agreement about the range of experiences and development opportunities which should be essential components of the preparation of headship. Hall *et al* underlined the need in this way: the consequences of the complexity of headship in practice... make it hard to believe that any deputy head, however competent and wide the experience in that post, could be ready for elevation to headship without prior formal training nd management development.

The following outlines four areas are

professional development which might be required in an individual's 'professional development portfolio' as the preparation for headship. Appropriate developmental opportunities could be made available in a variety of ways but might also form the curriculum for a 'staff college *without walls*'. This concept implies a particular *process* that would prepare a person for headship but not a particular place where it would be delivered.

(i) Developing values and vision

It is vital that potential heads have an opportunity to step back and reflect on their own experience alongside the writings of the great educators, the philosophers of education and those with a wiser interest in the ethics of management, e.g. Blanchard and Peale. This would help them to clarify and articulate their own educational and personal values. Such a process would prepare heads to share their vision for a school with the local community and, following consultation, to write the school's mission statement.

(ii) Developing the 'leading professional' - the educator sub-role

Future heads would also be expected to produce evidence of experience and professional development in the key area affecting schools and education. For example this might include : leading a team in successful planning and implementing a significant aspect of institutional change; training and/or experience in the fallowing areas—classroom observation and staff appraisal; styles of teaching and learning; financial planning and resource management; staff recruitment and development; public relations and community education; work with governors; the law as it affects the education service; curriculum planning, staffing and timetabling; approaches to assessment and the evaluation of performance; student guidance; knowledge of the research on effective schools.

(iii) Developing the 'chief executive'-the manager sub-role

This aspect of preparation for headship would focus on the generic management competencies required by heads and would include participation in an assessment centre with subsequent management development. The relatively objective evidence about performance that is provided by assessment centres should, in particular, boost the chances for further promotion of groups currently under-represented in senior positions. Management development would also power an understanding of team-building, the role played by individuals as team members, and an analysis of personal preferences in terms of team roles. The latter insight should assist with building 'balanced' teams of staff wherever possible. During this aspect of their professional development, potential heads would also gain an understanding of situational leadership.

(iv) developing a broader view - experience outside education

It might not be possible to make this a compulsory element in the preparation for headship, but all those with the ambition for headship should be strongly encouraged to gain some experience outside education. Ideally this would take the form of an extended project during a period of secondment for senior staff before headship. More limited opportunities for experience outside education could be made available, for example by providing additional non-contact time for a local placement during term-time, a short (one or two week) placement during a school holiday or occasional work-shadowing. It would also give potential heads a valuable opportunity to examine approaches to leadership and management in a different context and, in particular, important concepts like total quality management.

Preparation for leadership in all four of the areas outlined above would be supported by line-members and, at senior level, by heads. Training should be provided for them in the skills of coaching and mentoring so that their support role for professional development and career planning is a s effective as possible. It would also ensure that the main focus for development was 'on the job' experience.

A natural extension to this more coherent and comprehensive programme of professional development for leadership would be the on-going in-service educations and training of existing heads. Their own development would be enriched if they contributed to the preparation for headship by,m for example, training assessors at assessment centres, acting as coaches and mentors or helping with induction programmes for newly appointed heads. By helping in these ways they would also broaden and up-date their own skills and knowledge.

It is also assumed that the type of progarmme proposed as a preparation for headship would be undertaken, and the professional development portfolio assembled, over several years. The process would commence early in the career of a potential head. Ideally, appropriate elements would have been completed before promotion to a team leadership role at middle management level such as head of department or head of year.

Some practical considerations

The implementation of the strategies above and recommendations in these sections does, of course beg a number of important practical questions if we are to see a more coherent approach to school management development in the UK.

Where will the time be found?

All staff in schools are under immense pressure of work at the present time and it seems unlikely that his pressure will decrease, at least in the foreseeable future. There is also a legitimate and growing concern about staff taking time out of school for their own development became a low priority and began to suffer from neglect. However caution is urged in drawing this conclusion and allowing such a scenario to become the reality. It is precisely when an organizational system is under most pressure that time must be found for professional development otherwise the system risks going into decline.

In response to those who might respond by saying, 'But we have no time..', it is suggested that time might be found in the following ways. First, by making professional development a higher institutional and personal priority. Second, by making better use of the five in-service education and training days which are now part of the school year. Third, by giving up at least an equivalent amount of one's own time for personal professional development. Fourth, by proposing that a small proportion of the school budget is used to enhance staffing so that there can be an increase in non-contact time to be earmarked for professional development.

It is most important that the senior team takes the lead in making professional development a high institutional priority. They must also find their own space. The Secondary Heads Association publication, *'If it moves .... a study of the role of the Deputy Head'*, provided a clear indictment of the quite ludicrous, and often trivial, workload which was the daily grind of most deputy heads. How on earth can senior teams undertake their critical responsibilities for matters like strategic planning, evaluation and staff development if the deputies are worn out with the minutiae which should be done by other people?

Where will the money come from?

Although central government should continue to make the funding of management development in the education service a high priority, thee will never be enough money for all that is desirable. Following the introduction of local financial management more money is now getting directly into schools where senior teams and staff development committees can make the appropriate decisions about how it is spent. Hopefully they will be involved in local staff development networks so that resources are not wasted, for example, by 'reinventing wheels' or duplicating specialist forms of training. To allow sufficient development opportunities to be made available governors and heads will need to allocate a reasonable proportion of the school budget to staff (and their own) development.

It is most important that some of the money for staff development is retained and ear-marked at local, regional and/or national levels for the wider needs of the service like senior staff development. There is a real danger that if all the money ends up in schools then little, if any, will be allocated to these wider needs.

How will management development be delivered?

As much as the sources of funding for staff (and management) development are being fragmented within the education service, so is the means of delivery. Clearly, there is enormous potential for self-help from within a school. Too often people organizing development and training opportunities pay substantial sum of money to 'but in' expertise when equivalent taken (or better) is thee under their noses within the staff-room. So schools must keep an up-to-date inventory of the training and development skills available from within - another job for the staff development committee! Staff should be paid an appropriate fee even if it is for preparing a programme or materials for the professional development of their own colleagues.

Beyond of school itself, one should look to the local area for suitable expertise. This might be another school, a local business, the LEA or an institute of higher education. Then there is the wider scene of regional and national providers like professional associations, industry, private companies, consultants and, again, higher education.

To help make appropriate decisions about the right way to meet a particular professional development need, whether it is for a team or an individual, use should be made of local and regional networks. These can helpfully perform co-ordinating, quality control and information dissemination roles as direct outcomes of the type of strategic planning described [at the beginning] of this chapter.

Two final practical points should be considered when planning the delivery of management development,. First, aim for the right balance between school focussed (and inevitably inward-looking) development and opportunities to get out of the institution to meet people with different experience who work in different contexts. Second, although the number of management development providers, particularly commercial organization as and independent consultants, has been rapidly increasing, there has not been an equivalent improvement in quality.

How will professional development be accredited?

Management development opportunities range between the experience gained from reading a relevant book, going to an evening lecture, or doing something;differently on the job, to completing a six-year doctoral degree. Across this range and between these extremes, there is a wide variety of existing accreditation including various certificates, diplomas, degrees and higher degrees. Despite attempts like the Management Charter Initiative to rationalize management development and its accreditation for all occupations and professions, it seem both likely and desirable that there will continue to be some diversity in future provision.

If one accepts diversity as the likely reality, then one of the most sensible, and attractive ways ahead is to implement the idea of a 'professional development portfolio' (PDP) for all teachers. The PDP would be a similar document to the record of achievement for students. It would be issued at the start of a teacher's career, be recognized by both the profession and government (through the General Teaching Council and the Department of Education) and provide a flexible format for evidence of professional development within an agreed framework.

The frame work might include the four areas described in 'Coherence in the preparation for leadership' plus two additional sections to cover a curriculum vitae and a personal log of important experiences and achievements.

The PDP would be the property of an individual but that person would be encouraged to keep it up-to-date, to use it for career planning and professional development and to make it available as a component of job applications. An important feature of the PDP would be items of accreditation like certificates, diplomas and degrees just as a component of a record of achievement might be public examination certificates. It would also provide opportunities for the teacher to record their own evidence about books read, short courses attended, training undertaken and experience gained.

However there does remain an urgent need to improve the structure and accreditation of formal management development courses and qualifications so that it will be possible in future to meet two requirements. First, to introduce sufficient modularity to courses so that transfer fan be made between courses and levels without having to repeat components that have already been covered. Second, to acknowledge the relevance of prior learning and experience to decisions about the next appropriate step in an individual's professional development. Acceptable prior learning and experience should not be limited to formal courses and qualifications and should allow an individual to leap-frog lower level qualifications.

It almost goes without saying that applicants for senior posts, like deputy headships and headhsips, would be expected to have a very full and comprehensive PDP including both a wide range of experience and appropriate formal qualifications. But at the same time the PDP need not become a straight-jacket because the type of experience and qualifications that one would look for in the PDP of a potential deputy or head could change as the demands on senior staff in the future change. Equally, the availability and use of the PDP should provide a stimulus for personal and professional growth to teachers who did not necessarily want promotion to a more senior post.

Final thoughts

Management development - towards coherence?

If nothing else, the demands that legislation has placed on schools must raise school management development to the top of the educational agenda. It seems unlikely that the rate of change in society will slow down. Therefore schools must continually review and adapt their purposes, working practices and procedures for staff development in order to remain relevant to society's needs and successful in delivering society's expectations. Effective management will be a cornerstone of such relevance and success. Schools, local authorities and government must therefore make explicit their commitment to coherent strategies for management development at all levels in the service.

Despite the forces which are at present fragment ding the education service and the possibility of a more confused short-term future, coherent long-term strategies for management development are emerging. Hopefully this chapter has produced some evidence to support this optimistic view.

Management development - is that all?

Having underlined the central role of effective management development in successful schools, I close with the thought that it is only a means to an end. That end has three parts,. First, learning of high quality for the children and young people in the school community. Second, a programme of staff development which motivates all the staff to create the right conditions for this learning to take place. Third, leadership which inspires the commitment of staff and pupils alike to education as an exciting and life-long enterprise.

8 Quality in Further Education: An Unchanging Agenda

The initiative

The overall aim of the initiative is to link the demands for accountability with the desire for improvement; often they are seen to be mutually incompatible. Improving can be a statistical exercise, fulfilling requirements in terms of performance indicators but, when linked to the qualitative process of developing a narrative related to classroom practice, the two processes can be both developmental and powerful. A keynote of the Initiative is to gain the commitment of identified teams of staff in FE colleges to the idea of monitoring and evaluation as a positive and educative process in itself. Too often, quality is associated only with audit, review and inspection. If quality is genuinely in-built and integral to the whole institution, the integrity of the process may eliminate the fault-finding, problem-solving focus of many quality systems.

The identified teams are asked to work through 20 tasks in the handbook over one year. This is supported by systematic staff development and accredited training in evaluation techniques for team leaders. The teams identify 'quality gaps' in the area of provision for which they are responsible. These 'gaps' are then converted to quality targets that are tackled by the team itself. Nationally each team will identify 3 targets to be met each term. In order to address these targets, the team formulates an action plan identifying what is to be tackled, by whom, how and where. This provides the basis for a bid to a central college group which will then approve or modify the bid for funding. The funding may take the form of release time, equipment or materials. This forms the basis of reciprocal contracting - where the team contracts to deliver on its targets. The Senior management team would contract to deliver on its targets in the same way as all other teams.

All targets and time scales are 'public knowledge' and conform to the College strategic framework for quality. This means that the College Development Plan can be enacted through the contracting process and the regular review of progress each term.

Implementing the initiative

The first stage is to agree some key principles that provide the focus of improvement. Many teams include classroom practice, the quality of teaching and learning or the interaction between lecture and students. These concepts need to be dis-aggregated into a series of developmental tasks. At this stage, it is useful to being the process of identifying critical success factors or criteria for making judgements about the success of the improvement process. Although a necessarily lengthy process, it is essential to ensure a commitment through ownership - the team decides what the issues are, and what the criteria for success will be. The accredited training programme provides the necessary support for key individuals to lead the programme as 'professional evaluation'.

It is important that the central group that receives bids from teams undertakes a monitoring and evaluation role for the whole college. This Curriculum Review and Development Group is normally representative of all levels of staffing and operates rotation of membership to ensure full representation over several years. The CRDG remit is based on the College Development Plan and Quality Development strategy for the institution. Team progress is monitored by brief half-termly reporting and end of term reviews.

The reciprocal contracting of the TQM system extends to learner contracts as an integral part of "entitlement". This replicates a work contract for students and would include enhanced opportunities for learner support and study skills programmes.

Methodology of the initiative

The methodology of the initiative is based on the work of David Kolb and D A Schon. This model of experimental learning and the reflective practitioner, exemplified through the research and development function, is not usually part of the FE College system. If time for 'reflection' is built into the teaching and learning programme, it becomes possible to identify needs and meet planning requirements within "normal practice". The teams therefore use a variety of monitoring and evaluation techniques, each suited to its own purpose. The widespread use of questionnaires is generally found to be of limited use. Both students and staff can become "anaesthetised" to their use and the quality of some information is doubtful. By using a variety of methods, it is possible to triangulate on issues, and gain a much closer insight into the origins and nature of the issues. Many of the so-called problems identified by some quality systems are products of the system itself rather than being symptomatic of real underling course culture.

Evaluation techniques can be built into learning programmes, using tutorials, seminars and workshops. The common complaint is that "we don't have time...(for quality)." Teaching hours are being reduced and many staff are under considerable stress as a direct result of increased administration. A possible solution lies in revisiting teaching methodologies, timetabling and room allocations. It becomes necessary for the team to have increasing ownership of the means to deliver the curriculum that meet their identified needs and the needs of the students more effectively.

Traditionally colleges have been driven by SSRs and the requirements of resource allocations based on student numbers. Increasingly, the notion of performance related funding may produce a more efficient and effective way of delivering learning programmes that will incorporate "self-critical academic maturity". These are the issues that can be picked up very quickly by the 'empowered' course team. Their initial solutions to perceive problems may be crude, but they offer a genuine R and D function that many commercial operations value highly. the emphasis on discrete elements of college operations eg. marketing, recruitment, quality, tends to fragment and dispel responses such as - "its someone else's responsibility". You cannot delegate or subcontract quality and the fundamental approach of TQM lies in a set of values and attitudes that embody commitment to continuous improvement. In the same way, quality is not a project, nor is it a standard to be achieved. This serves only to limit achievement and leads to a "lip-service"model of the way that things should be done.

Quality improvement

The "steps" to quality improvement begin with a view about "what do we mean by quality". Programme Area teams may have a different view to that of the management teams; providing interesting perspectives on the college's view of quality. Agreeing common principles is part of the first reflective stage. It is based primarily on experience (as in the Kolb model), and may be a function of a series of critical incidents, concerns, problems, good ideas or hunches.

These form the basis of the keynote principles to be outlines in the college Quality Development Action Plan, that outlines the "mission" and incorporates commitment to specific quality attributes.

Secondly, decisions about the composition of teams will provide a basis for identifying areas of "common effort". In itself an interesting exercise, this can identify the "black holes" of provision and the "team that never meets" or the "team that never was". Team forming provides a basis for more collaborative working and for improved communications and shared resources. Indeed, the benefits of this single exercise often promote a more integrative approach to all aspects of the college provision and lead to consideration of structured responses.

The third stage is for each team to identify their own response to "quality gaps", as perceived by the team. These gaps should become targets for improvement, recognising that in some cases there are resource implications for management attention. Initially, it is useful to identify smaller (incremental) issues for improvement, rather than medium or long term targets. If all teams engage in the process, by contracting to deliver, the whole college can move rapidly to a stage of critical mass. At this point the management strategy should incorporate a moderating influence, ensuring a degree of realism and consistency in both targeting and methodology. This is important to ensure that diversity of approach does not preclude a corporateness of purpose.

It would be possible for a system to be "bought in" but this does not generally engender ownership or indeed, commitment by all. Most alternatives are superstructures rather than infrastructures - built on, rather than built in. It is essential to grow the system within the organisation rather than impose a structure for accountability; this is because the reaction to the exogenous system is often to subvert or at least to ignore it. Systems for accountability can often be counter productive, generating whole sub-systems and consuming large amounts of time and energy.

9 Concept of Quality

The concept of quality

Quality has a variety of contradictory meanings. As Naomi Pfeffer and Anna Coote have observed in their discussion of quality in the welfare services 'Quality' is a slippery concept'. It implies different things to different people. Everyone is in favour of providing quality education. The arguments start because there is a lack of agreement as to what it means. It is, therefore, necessary to have a clear understanding of the various meanings of quality otherwise there is a danger that it becomes a mere catchphrase, a word with high moral tone but little practical value. understanding of the diverse meanings of quality is a necessary starting point for our discussion of TQM.

A possible reason for the enigmatic nature of quality is that it is a dynamic idea.The emotional and moral force which quality possesses makes it a difficult idea to tie down. There is the danger that much of its vitality can be lost if it is subjected to too much academic analysis. Westley and Mintzberg make the point that this happens to many important concepts which are freely used in practical settings.

A strange process seems to occur as concepts such as culture and charisma (and we can add quality) move from practice to academic research. Loosely used in practice, these concepts, as they enter academia become subjected to a concerted effort to force them to lie down and behave, to render them properly scientific. In the process they seem to lose emotional resonance, no longer expressing the reality that practitioners tried to capture.

Quality is a dynamic idea and exact definitions are not particularly helpful.However, its range of meanings does cause confusion. Important practical consequences flow from these different meanings. For this reason they need discussion.

Quality as an absolute concept

Some of the confusion over the meaning of quality arises because it can be used both as an absolute and a relative concept. Quality in everyday conversation is mainly used as an absolute. People use it to describe expensive restaurants and luxury cars. As an absolute, quality is similar in nature to goodness, beauty, and truth; an ideal with which there can be no compromise. In the absolute definition this which exhibit quality are of the highest possible standard which cannot be surpassed.Quality products are things of perfection made with no expense spared. They are valuable and convey prestige to their owners. 'Quality cars', for example, are hand-built and expensive and have interiors of walnut and leather. Rarity and expense are two the features of quality in this definition. Quality in this sense is used to convey status and positional advantage, and the ownership of things of 'quality' sets their owners apart from those who cannot afford them. It is synonymous with 'high quality or top quality'. To use the words of Pfeffer and Coote again, 'Most of us admire it, many of us want it, few of us can have it' (Pfeffer and Coote, 1991, p4). Used in the educational context this concept of quality is essentially elitist. By definition only a few institutions are able to offer such a 'high quality' educational experience to their learners. Most learners cannot afford it, and most institutions cannot aspire to provide it.The absolute notions of 'high quality' have little to do with TQM. However, the absolute meaning often sticks in discussions of TQM. So when addressing quality in its technical, TQM, sense there is still an aura of luxury and status about it. Quality has class. This subtle and often subliminal use of language can be useful for public relations purpose, and may help an educational institutions promote ideas of quality. It also demonstrates that pursuing quality is all about performing to the highest standards.

The relative concept of quality

Quality can also be employed as a relative concept. This is the sense in which it is used in TQM. The relative definition views quality not as an attribute of a product or service, but as something which is ascribed to it. Quality can be judged to exist when a good or service meets the specification that has been laid down for it. Quality is not the end in itself, but a means by which the end product is judged to be up to standard. Quality products or services, in this relative or ascribed definition need not be expensive and exclusive. They may be beautiful, but not necessarily so. They donot have to be special. They can be ordinary, commonplace, and familiar. Overhead projectors, ballpoint pens, and the school catering service may all exhibit quality if they meet simple but crucially important standards. They must do what they claim to do, and do what their customers expect of them. In other words they must be 'fit for their purpose', as the British Standards Institution defines quality.

The relative definition of quality has two aspects to it. The first is measuring up to specification. The second is meeting customer requirements. The first usage-measuring up-is often summed up as 'fitness for purpose or use'. This is sometimes called the producer definition of quality. Quality for the producer is achieved by its products or services meeting a pre-defined specification in a consistent fashion. Quality is demonstrated by a producer having a system, known as a quality assurance system, which enables the consistent production of the good or service to a particular standard or specification. A product exhibits quality so long as it consistently meets its maker's claims for it.

In this definition both Rover cars and Rolls-Royces are quality products. Luxury, beauty, exclusivity and price do not enter into the equation. So long as products conform to their manufacturers' specifications and standards they exhibit quality. This view of quality is sometimes called 'quality in fact'. 'Quality in fact' is the basis of the quality assurance systems devised in accordance with the British Standards Institution in the BS5750 standard or the identical international standard ISO9000.

The consumer definition of quality

Who should decide whether a school or college is providing a quality service? The answer will tell us much about the values and aspirations of the institution. It is essential to have a clear idea of who is ascribing the attribute of quality; is it the producer or the consumer? The reason for posing this question is because the views of producers and consumers are not always identical. It does happen that perfectly good and useful products and services are rejected by consumers. Making a product to specification does not guarantee sales. A different version of the ascribed view of quality is needed to take account of this problem.

Organizations who follow the TQM path regard quality as being defined by their customers. The reason for this is simple. Customers are the final arbitrators of quality and without them the institution does not exist. The TQM institution has to use all means at its disposal to explore its customers' requirements. Total quality means knowing them in ways and depths never fully explored before and using this knowledge to translate needs into innovative new products and business approaches'.

Quality can be defined as that which best satisfies and exceeds customers needs and wants. This is sometimes called 'quality in perception'. Quality can be said to lie in the eyes of the beholder. This is a very important and powerful definition, and one that any institution ignores at its peril. It is the consumers who make the judgement on quality, which they do by reference to the best comparable performer.

Tom Peters, discussing the pivotal role of the consumer in quality in *Thriving On Chaos*, argues that the *perceived* quality of a business 's product or service is the most important single factor affecting its performance. Peters argues that quality as defined by the customer is more important than price in determining the demand for a majority of good and services.His unequivocal findings are that customers will always pay more for the best quality,regardless of the type of product. He has also found that employees become energized when they have the opportunity to provide a quality service or produce a quality product. However, he does sound a warning because new entrants to the market will also be redefining quality to the customer.

Quality control, quality assurance, and total quality

As well as providing a definition of quality it is necessary to understand the difference between three other important quality ideas. These are the distinctions which are made between quality control, quality assurance and total quality.

Quality Control is historically the oldest concept. It involves the detection and elimination of components or final products which are not up to standard. It is an after-the-event process concerned with detecting and rejecting defective items. As a method of ensuring quality it may involve a considerable amount of waste, scrap and reworking. Quality control is usually carried out by quality professionals known as quality controllers or inspectors. Inspection and testing are the most common methods of quality control, and are widely used in education to determine whether standards are being met.

Quality assurance is different from quality control. It is before and during -the-event process. Its concern is to prevent faults occurring in the first place. Quality is designed into the process to attempt to ensure that the product is produced to a predetermined specification. Simply, quality assurance is a means of producing defect-and fault-free products. The aim, in the words of Philip B Crosby, is 'zero defects'. Quality assurance is about consistently meeting product specification or getting things 'right first time, every time'. Quality assurance is made the responsibility of the workforce, usually working in cells or teams, rather than the inspector, although inspection can have a role to play in quality assurance. The quality of the good or service is assured by there being a system, which lays down exactly how production should take place and to what standards.Quality standards are maintained by following the procedures laid down in the QA system.

Total quality management incorporates quality assurance, and extend and develops it. TQM is about creating a quality culture where the aim of every member of staff is to delight their customers, and where the structure of their organization allows them to do so. In the total quality definition of quality the customer is sovereign.It is the approach popularized by Peters and Waterman in *In Search of Excellence*, and which has been a constant theme of Tom Peters' writings since. Many companies, such as Marks and Spencer, British Airways, and Sainsburys have been pursuing this approach for a number of years. It is about providing the customer with what they want, when they want it and how they want it. It involves moving with changing customer expectations and fashions to design products and services which meet and exceed their expectations. Only by delighting customers will they return and tell their friends about it. The perceptions and expectations of customers are recognized as being short-term and fickle, and so organizations have to find ways of keeping close to their customers to be able to respond to their changing tastes, needs and wants.

The 'product' of education

It is always necessary to ask two fundamental questions when trying to understand quality in any station. The first is, what is the product? and the second is, who are the customers? These questions are equally applicable to the discussion of quality in education.

What is the product of education? There are a number of different candidates for this title. The pupil or the student is often spoken about as if they are the product. In education we often talk as though learners are the output, especially with reference to the institution's perceived performance over discipline and behaviour. Terms like 'the supply of graduates' make education sound like a production line with students emerging from the end of it. The problem with this definition is that it is difficult to square it with much educational practice.

For a product to be the subject of quality assurance process the producer needs firstly to specify and control the source of supply. Secondly, the 'raw material' must pass through a standard process or set of processes, and the output must meet defined specifications. Such a model does not easily fit education, although there are those that might wish that it would. Such a model would clearly require an initial selection of learners to be made. Some sectors of education do this, but many, following the comprehensive principle of open access, do not. However, it is from there on that the analogy begins to fall apart. While processes such as the national curriculum and the specification of standards and competencies in NVQs have improved the standardization of the process, nevertheless the process of education is anything but uniform.

It is impossible to produce pupils and students to any particular guaranteed standard. As Lynton Gray has put it in his very useful discussion of the issue: 'Human beings are notoriously non-standards, and they bring into educational situations a range of experiences, emotions and opinions which cannot be kept in the background of the operation. Judging quality is very different from inspecting the output of a factory, or judging the service provided by a retail outlet. The idea of the learner as the product misses the complexities of the learning process and the uniqueness of each individual learner.

How, then, do we define the product? Rather than answer this directly it is more helpful to view education as a service rather than a production line. The distinction between a product and a service is important because there are fundamental differences between them which have a bearing on how their quality can be assured.

Service quality

Service quality characteristics are more difficult to

define than those for physical products. This is because they include many important subjective elements.The causes of poor quality and quality failure are different for services and products. Products often fail because of faults in raw materials and components. Their design may be faulty or they may not be manufactured to specification. Poor quality services, on the other hand, are usually directly attributable to employee behaviors or attitude. They often result from lack of care or courtesy. Indifference, lack of training or concern are often principal reasons for a breakdown of service. The different nature of service quality characteristics needs to be borne in mind when discussing educational quality.

Service differ from production in a number of important ways. They are major differences between delivering a service and manufacturing goods.The first difference between the tow is that services usually involve direct contact between the provider and the end-users. Services are delivered directly by people to people. There is a close relationship between the customer and the person who delivers the service. The service cannot be separated from the person delivering it or from the person receiving it. Every interaction is different, and the quality of the interaction is in part determined by the customer. The quality of the service is determined both by the person delivering the person receiving the service. Unlike production there can be no absolute consistency or homogeneity in service delivery. The consistency of the service can only be within boundaries.

Time is the second important element of service quality.Services have to be delivered on time, and this is as important as their physical specification. Additionally, as a service is consumed at the moment of delivery the control of its quality by inspection is always too late. The close personal interactions found in services allow multiple opportunities for feedback and evaluation and these provide the main, but not the only, means of judging whether customers are satisfied with it.

The third differences is that unlike a product, a service cannot be serviced or mended. A poor meal is a poor meal. It cannot be repaired. For this reason it is important that the standard of services should be right first time every time. Paradoxically, it is the high possibility of human error and failing that makes is difficult, if not impossible, to achieve the right first time standard. Nevertheless, this should always be the aim.

Fourth, services face the problem of intangibility. It is often difficult to describe to potential customers exactly what is being offered. It is equally difficult on occasions for customers to describe what they want from the service. Services are largely about process rather than product. It is usually more important how an outcome is arrived at than what the outcome is.

The fact that services are usually rendered directly to customers by junior employees is the fifth distinguishing feature of a service. Senior staff are generally remote from customers. Most customers never have access to senior managers. The quality of the initial interactions colors the view customers have of the whole organization, and so the organization has to find ways of motivating front-line employees to always deliver of their best. This is why training and staff development are crucial importance. While senior managers may not serve at the front in service organizations they must lead from the front and convey to their staff their vision of the service and the standards they want set for it.

Lastly, it is very difficult to measure successful output and productivity in services. The only meaningful performance indicators are those of customer satisfaction. Intangibles or 'soft' measures are often as important to success and to the customer as are hard and objective performance indicators. 'Soft' indicators - care, courtesy, concern, friendliness, and helpfulness- are often uppermost in customers' minds. Intangibility makes it very difficult to turn round poor service, because it is sometimes impossible to convince dissatisfied customers that a service has changed for the better. Consumers judge quality by comparing their perceptions of what they receive with their expectations of it. Much of this is also true for education. Reputation is crucial to an institutions' success, but the origin of that reputation often defies analysis and measurement. What we do know is that reputation has a great deal to do with the care and concern shown to pupils and students.

For the purposes of analysing quality it is more appropriate to view education as a service industry than as a production process. Once this view is established the institution needs to define clearly the service it is providing and the standards to which they will be delivered. This needs to be carried out in conjunction with all its customer groups, including discussions with governors, parents, and with industry directly or via local Education Business Partnerships.

Education and its customers

We have defined education as a provider of services. Those services include tuition, assessment, and guidance to pupils and students, their parents and sponsors. The customers-the stakeholders of the service-are a very diverse group and need identifying. If quality is about meeting and exceeding customer needs and wants it is important to be clear whose needs and wants we should be satisfying.

It is at this point important to say something about the idea of a 'customer' in the context of education. To some educationalists 'customer' has a distinctly commercial tone which is not applicable to education. The prefer to use client instead. Client, with its connotations or professional service is seen as more appropriate. Stakeholder is another term often used in this context. Others reject all such language and would rather stay with pupil or student. Language is important if an idea is to be acceptable.In this book customer and learner are mainly employed, but there is no quarrel with those who might wish to substitute other terms.

There are others who should make a distinction between 'clients' who are the primary beneficiaries of the education service, and 'customers', who are those who pay for it but who may be at one remove, such as parents, governors, employers or government. In this book customers will be used for both sets of relationships and the distinction will be made between 'primary customers' who directly receive the service, 'secondary customers' such as parents, governors, sponsoring employers of FE students who have a direct stake in the education of a particular individual or in a particular institution, and 'teritiary customers' who have less direct but none the less crucial stakeholding in education such as future employers, government and society as a whole. To some extent this distinction is at odds with schools' legislation. The 1988 Education Reform Act makes the parents the primary customers of the process. This provides an additional, but not irreconcilable, difficulty for schools. The diversity of customers makes it all the more important for educational institutions to focus on customer wants and to develop mechanisms for responding to them. It is important to define clearly the nature of the service an institution provides to its customers.It is equally important to maintain an excellent and continuing dialogue with them. The best form of marketing is that which the learners do on its behalf. Their successes are also the institutions.

Internal educational customers

While the major focus of any school, college or university must be on its external customers-learners, parents, etc—it is important to remember that everyone working in an institutions provides services to their colleagues. In TQM staff members are known as internal customers. Poor internal relationships prevent an institution working properly, and in the end it is the external customers who suffer.

10 Total Quality Management in Education

The reforms of the education service in the 1980s provide the most fundamental challenges to the prevailing orthodoxies of the management of educational institutions. The changes are so profound that any attempt to respond to them using established principles and processes is likely to be dysfunctional. At the same time there is a critical need to establish a moral basis for educational management so that the demands of the reforms do not result in pragmatic and expedient responses. This chapter argues that total Quality Management (TQM) offers a vehicle for schools and colleges to manage themselves effectively in a time of rapid change and retain a clear focus on the essential and dominant purposes of education.

The Education Reform Act 1988 and related legislation Scotland and Northern Ireland has had the net effect of shifting responsibility, authority and accountability to the institutional level, eroding the traditional infrastructure of support and focusing on to individual institutions the previously diffuse patterns of management activity. In essence the changes are encapsulated in the concept of the 'self-governing' school or college. The specific requirements on schools in England and Wales to manage the national curriculum LMS and appraisal in the context of parental choice and the impact of incorporation on post-compulsory institutions create demands which are of a different order of magnitude to anything previously encountered. The possibility of institutions *not* managing themselves has now been removed as an option. In the context of consumer choice failing institutions will be allowed the ultimate failure.

A further factor is the changing culture in which schools and colleges will have to operate. As the quality movement extends into the commercial and public sectors so expectations on all providers will change. Parents will increasingly be working in TQM companies, school-leavers and students will be seeking employment in organizations managed according to quality criteria. There will inevitably be increasingly specific demands on schools and colleges as suppliers. Most readers will be familiar with the British Standard 'kitemark'; as well as being an indication of safety, there is a kitemark for quality management systems, BS 5750. Some further education colleges are having to seek BS 5750 accreditation in order to be able to deal with registered companies.

Sallis has identified four imperatives for change which he argues point towards a total quality approach. The professional imperative implies a commitment to client needs and the obligation to meet those needs by deploying knowledge and skills to best effect., The moral imperative is the need to find a basis for management action which is firmly rooted in the key purposes of educational institutions. Quality approaches are offered as a way of meeting long-standing concerns about the nature of management in schools and colleges. Sallis extends the applicability of TQM to education by arguing that there are two further imperatives operating, the competitive and survival. These are closely linked but in essence the emergence of a market economy in education requires the evolution of strategies which reconcile the first two imperatives with the need to ensure institutional viability.

There is a need for educational institutions to develop a sophisticated response to this new climate. On the one hand this has profound dangers in that schools and colleges might be seduced into adopting structures and procedures which convey a veneer of efficiency but which lose sight of the key purposes of educational institutions. There is the danger of the triumph of the 'men in grey suits'-a situation where administration becomes a substitute for managing and where power relationships replace professional relationships. Shipman characterizes the issue in the following terms:

> By concentrating school management on top-down procedures, training has missed both the opportunity to help teachers raise standards and to use their interest in helping children learn... By the late 1980s, Management literature outside education was stressing not only the importance of vision at the top, but of the need to encourage initiative at all levels of the organization. Yet there is still no sign of any shift around management training in education. The stress is still on means confused with ends and on administration not management.

The combination of the need to respond to the 1988 Act and preserve the integrity of the learning process is further complicated by a third factor-the concern with quality. The issue of quality in education is perennial one and the standard response has been in Platonic terms-to see it as an intellectual problem to be grappled with which, buy definition, is probably not capable of solutions. Quality has been perceived as an ideal, an absolute like truth, justice and beauty which we can only ever aspire to. The definition of quality in education is for philosopher-kings and not for children, parents or teachers!

This approach is no longer acceptable, appropriate or desirable. Changing social expectations, the concept of 'rights' being expressed in practical terms, the emergence of a culture of expectation where customer needs are paramount, mean that institutions have to be in a dynamic interaction with those for whom they are created to provide a service. The shift is from quality as an ideal to be attained to quality as a relationship to be managed. For industry and commerce, and increasingly for the public sector, TQM represents a powerful means of meeting this challenge. It is not possible to list all the organizations involved in the quality movement; evidence of increasing activity is to be found in the number of companies seeking BS 5750 accreditation, the number of public bodies adopting; TQM, the increasing levels of training provided and the volume of literature available. It will be for the reader to decide how far it is an appropriate response for schools and colleges. TQM has three crucial features which distinguish it from other theories of managing. Firstly, it is holistic, it permeates every aspect of an organization, every relationship and every process. It therefore offers an integrity and coherence which is lacking in most other models. Secondly, it is value driven: TQM places fundamental significance on values and purpose. It therefore introduces a moral imperative into management which would seem necessary in the context of the education of children and young people. Thirdly, it is about managing the interpersonal components of all organizations and equally acknowledges the interdependence between an organization and its environment.

The nature of TQM

The pedigree of TQM can be traced to the work of two Americans, Deming and Juran. Both approached the issue of quality from a background of statistics used in manufacturing processes in the engineering industry. Their work was first widely adopted in Japan, 'discovered' in the USA in the late 1970s and subsequently (as often is the case) in Britain in the early 1980s. Deming and Juran extended the original base of their work into all aspects or organizational management and their foundations have been built on by a number of practitioner-writers, notably Crosby (1979). The impact of their ideas can be found in the origins of manufactured goods in households and garages across Britain, for the dominance of imported consumer goods, notably Japanese in origin, can be largely explained in terms of quality.

There is not a single, homogeneous theory of TQM. The 'gurus" and their disciples have produced sets of percepts which are broadly in accord but differ in significant respects. Most importantly TQM has to evolve in response to the needs, context and values of a specific organization. There will therefore be significant differences between an engineering company an airline, a retail organization and public sector activities in the way in which TQM is interpreted and applied. However, certain fundamental principle will remain constant and these can be identified by synthesizing the key imperative of the originators of TQM:

(1) The definition of quality is that of the customer, not the supplier.

(2) Customers are defined as anyone who receives a product or service, i.e. they are internal and external to the organization and not just the 'person who pays'.

(3) Quality consists of meeting stated needs, requirements and standards.

(4) Quality is achieved by the prevention of work that does not meet standards; not by the detection of failure but by continuously improving the service or product.

(5) The move to qualify is driven by senior management but is the responsibility of those in the organization; qualify has to be 'built in' to every process.

(6) Quality is measured by statistical processes, the cost of quality is the cost of non-conformance with stated requirements, the 'gap' between expectation and delivery.

(7) The most powerful vehicle for ensuring quality relationship is the effective team.

(8) Education and training are fundamental to the quality organization.

These components demonstrate the factors in understanding the relationship between TQM and quality control and quality assurance. Quality control is a well-established practice in most industrial concerns; it involves monitoring, checking and controlling, i.e. inspection. Control is a historic activity: it takes place after the even and is carried out by a third party, not the producer. Responsibility is therefore removed from the person who actually makes the product. Quality assurance by contrast is anticipatory: standards and procedures are clearly defined in advance and the worker is trained to be able to meet them. This approach is best exemplified in BS 5750 which defines the processes deemed necessary to operate quality systems and deliver products which conform to customer requirements. TQM builds on quality assurance by extending the principles to every aspect of organizational life and not just the manufacturing or service process. TQM recognizes and respects the potential of every individual to be more than the extension of an operating procedure It also stresses the need for individual autonomy the need to feel in personal control and not a victim Workers know *what* they have to produce but are able to decide for themselves *how* to produce it TQM organizations outperform their rivals because they are better at identifying and meeting customer requirements and because they recognize that employees are customers with requirements as much as the recipients of products and services.

The customer

In the TQM organization the customer or client is defined as the person or group in receipt of a product or service. Thus the customer is not external to the organization but exists at every stage required to complete the manufacture of a product or delivery of a service. The most potent image is that of the 'chain' of customers, linked together by the process. Each 'sub-unit' or link exists only in relationship to other links; interdependence is the hallmark of TQM organizations.

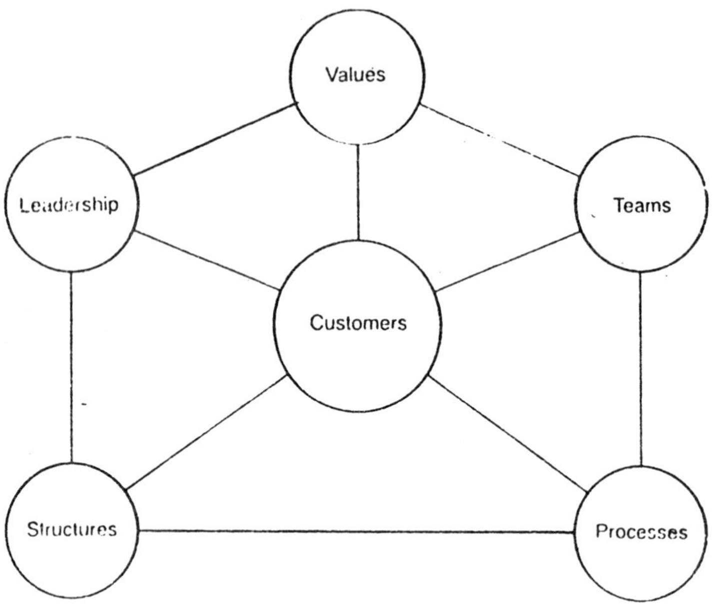

The components of TQM

Managing for quality requires organizations to find out customer requirements by asking and listening.

TQM requires listening organizations which ask the right questions of the right people and then act on the replies. A further crucial concept is that the organization only exists for its customers, it has no other purpose or justification. Many TQM companies have statements of philosophy which argue that quality comes before profit-the logic is simple: if customer needs are met then profitability is inevitable. TQM companies are obsessive about customer care and satisfaction because they have established a correlation between customer satisfaction, reducing costs and enhancing profitability.

In practical terms this means obtaining regular feed back to ensure that services are as required, for example that school prospectuses are written in appropriate language, teaching strategies are relevant and reports provide significant data. This implies regular monitoring and evaluation at each stage of the prevision of a product or service.

Values

What distinguishes TQM organizations from others is the emphasis on, and significance attached to, the values of the organization and the way in which the vision is communicated and permeates working relationships. Research in the commercial and educational sectors confirms that the most successful organizations have explicit and shared values which are not moral abstractions but the basis for decision-making and action. Mission is central to total quality management in that it:

- provides a sense of direction and purpose,
- acts as a unifying factor,

- provides criteria for decision-making,
- articulates values,
- ensures consistency of purpose,
- defines customers,
- characterizes the organization to its community,
- provides challenge and motivation.

One of the most powerful features of TQM is its high ethical content and the way in which principle is the basis for practice.

Schools and colleges almost always have aims and objectives, the issue is how far they are used as the basis for decision-making, notably in budget planning.

Leadership

If moral integrity is fundamental to TQM then leadership is the means by which it is expressed. Leadership is defined in the context of TQM as providing and driving the vision. TQM draws a sharp distinction between leading, managing and administering. Quality leadership has the following components.

(1) *Vision:* this is the clear view as to where the organization is going-the values, hopes and aspirations are actively communicated and used as the basis for action. Vision is not the monopoly of leadership but it is their primary responsibility to articulate it.

(2) *Creativity*: in order to make the vision live, leadership has to be creative; to find solutions to problems, to unravel complexity, to analyse

rather than describe and to generate solutions that address the issue. Thinking is therefore a crucial leadership activity.

(3) *Sensitivity:* this is a problematic area but in essence quality leadership is about the quality of personal relationships, consistency of behaviour and providing a personal model which is expressed in very specific skills : active listening, giving feedback, negotiating, giving praise, managing conflict, networking and empathizing.

(4) *Empowerment:* a fundamental characteristic of leadership in the context of TQM is the need to release the potential of individuals, allowing them to flourish and grow as people rather than as employees-to release their capacity for infinite improvement. Empowerment is given practical expression through delegation and training which allow the individual to develop personal responsibility and control. In essence the person is trusted through a belief in their capacity for growth.

(5) *Managing change*: the quality leader loves change, recognizes it as the abiding and dominant social dynamic and leads the organization so as to become changing rather than changed. This involves the creation of a learning organization which shifts from reaction to anticipation and which emphasizes appropriate behaviour as the basis for responding to the environment. The TQM organization integrates personal development into organizational development by enhancing personal capability. Leadership is not about preserving the status quo.

The leader of the TQM organization is, in essence, concerned about values and people, setting the direction and allowing people to achieve targets, being concerned with the macro and the micro. The issue for education is the extent to which leadership differentiated from management and administration. Torrington and Weightman discuss the problem in terms of the secondary school deputy head who spends 40% of her time on administration-which is defined as work that can be done by an intelligent 16-year-old. Management, by contrast, is concerned with implementing the vision, with translating principles into practice through planning, delegating, monitoring, budgeting and developing.

Teams

A team is a quality group. All the literature on teams stresses the importance of clarity of purpose and effective interpersonal relationships as the basis for effective teamwork. Both in theory and practice teams are seen as fundamental to the management of quality in organizations. Effective teams display the following characteristics :

- Explicit and shared values; the team has a common vocabulary and sense of direction.
- Situational leadership; the team is sufficiently mature to base leadership on function and need rather than power and status, skills are more important than hierarchical factors.
- Commitment; there is pride in team membership.
- Clear task; the outcome that the team is created to achieve is clear, realistic and understood.

- Review; effective teams learn and develop by a process of continuous feed-back and review.
- Openness; teams achieve a high level of candour in review and exchange.
- Collaboration; decisions are shared and have full commitment.
- Action; quality teams make thing happen.

Effective teams balance task and process-they get the job done, improve personal relationships and enhance individual members.

Quality circles are one of the best-known manifestations of the TQM movement. In essence they are teams established as part of the work process to improve operating procedures. Too often teams in schools and colleges are historical accidents and little though is given to their composition or development. There is often a substantial emphasis on task with little recognition of the importance of social issues.

Processes

A key feature of managing for quality is defining the components of work processes. This is where BS 5750 is particularly relevant. In essence, once customer requirements have been established then it is necessary to set up processes and procedures to ensure conformity to those requirements. In one sense it is necessary to minimize variation from the desired norm. BS 5750 identified the following components of managing processes:

- Systems should be established to manage all processes with the emphasis on prevention.

- Documentation should be produced including a quality manual which outlines procedures in detail and establishes record-keeping systems.
- The system should incorporate a feedback mechanisms to facilitate customer responses.
- Quality audits should take place to verify the implementation of the procedures.

In practical terms this means the specifying of 'correct procedures' so that conformance to requirements is an inevitable outcome rather than an aspiration. The way in which processes are managed centres on measurement. Measurement is used to ensure conformity to standards, to identify the cost of deviation and to monitor the efficiency of any improvements made to the process. Improving work processes is the means by which quality is delivered, processes are worked on to ensure that they produce goods and services which are closer to customer requirements and so add value, The cost of quality is not the cost of improving processes but the cost of not conforming to customer requirements. The management of this process is a useful exemplification of TQM in action, the most appropriate people to take the decisions about improving processes are those who are 'closest to the customer'. Thus the appropriate procedures are defined by those who have the responsibility to implement them but working to clear organizational guidelines. This principle is usefully illustrated by Handy who refers to the 'inverted do'nut'. The solid core of the do'nut is tightly specified and explicitly defines that which must be done. The outer ring is available for discretion, interpretation and local initiative. It is the outer ring which allows for individual and team autonomy whilst ensuring consistency and conformity to organizational goals and values.

The management of the quality process has to take into account three factors :

(1) The identification and communication of customer requirements.

(2) The identification and communication of demands on the supplier.

(3) The provision of skills, resources and procedures necessary to complete the process.

Unless the 'links in the chain' are clear the process cannot function. Education is very good at defining some key processes, notably the curriculum; management processes are not always as well established. The results of SATs and examinations can be used to modify teaching strategies as they can provide diagnostic data. If management processes are to be improved then there is a need to develop quantifiable outcomes which facilitate analysis of meetings, budgets, training, etc.

Structures

Organizations which attempt to introduce TQM without reviewing their structure are probably doomed to failure. Few organizations have structures which are customer focused, they tend to be based on formal hierarchies bound together by bureaucratic working practices.

The customer is often a 'nuisance', getting in the way of the machine running smoothly. The TQM organization aspires to meet the fallowing criteria:

- The whole organization is 'close' to the customer, suppliers talk directly to clients.
- Effective work teams are used as the basis for the structure rather than as incidental to it.
- The structure facilitates real delegation, teams and individuals are allowed maximum control of their work.
- The structure is a practical manifestation of the values of the organization.

The theoretical structure of the quality organization resembles a coalition of autonomous teams able to interact directly with customers and with each other, all linked to senior management teams responsible for strategy. However, the center holds only as much power as is necessary-authority and responsibility are delegated by senior management to teams commensurate with the task they have to do. There is no one model for the structure of a quality organizations; what is important is that the structure should facilitate task and process.

Most large schools and colleges work on a hierarchical structure; it is difficult to identify the educational, professional or management rationale for such an approach. The curriculum is delivered by subject teams. Schools and colleges function, usually, buy problem-solving coalitions that come together for a specific purpose. Quality organizations seek to reconcile form and function by having structures that reflect the reality of working relationships. The parallel structures for academic and pastoral systems in secondary schools are a classic example of form not matching function; most schools would argue that the academic and pastoral processes and structures are interdependent yet the actual organizational pattern denies this.

TQM in the context of education

It is difficult to find neat categorization of TQM in terms of theoretical models. Its origins are very much in an analysis of perceived success and the extrapolation of the factors contributing to that success. The model might therefore be conceived of a s a pragmatic one, i.e. theory is derived from practice and does not require intellectual legitimation. Indeed writers on quality frequently warn against the dangers of an overly 'academic' response to the principles enunciated; there are frequent cautions against 'paralysis by analysis'. TQM is perceived as management in action and organizational effectiveness is the sole legitimation.

There is, as yet, very little empirical evidence available on the impact of quality approaches in schools and colleges. Samuel provides useful indicators of some areas of school management that lend themselves to a TQM approach:

- the experience of pupils when taken by a supply teacher,
- the impact of the homework policy,
- consistency in entry criteria for the sixth form,
- heads of department being responsible for their work areas,
- response times for repairs and maintenance.

However, in reviewing the applicability of TQM to the education service it is helpful to see how it relates to existing analytical models. In its stress upon organizational goals, the central importance of leadership and the importance of establishing systems to manage processes TQM coincides with the formal models of management outlined by Bush. However, the applicability of the bureaucratic model is immediately challenged by the emphasis on teams, social processes and the empowering and developmental model of leadership. There is no doubt that the individual is subordinated to the organization in terms of values but the TQM organization then accepts the need to secure the commitment and personal involvement of the individual, i.e. there is no question of denying personal integrity. There is also a recognition that values are only given expression through individual action.

The emphasis on teams raises the issue of democratic and collegial models. The criteria for effective teams are highly reminiscent of the characteristics of collegiality as outlined by Bush. The requirement for open decision-making, and the emphasis on individual responses to the organization all appear to locate TQM firmly in a human relations view of management. It may well be that TQM represents the next generation of thinking in management theory where the criteria are practical rather than ideological. TQM represents a form of conceptual pluralism, i.e. it does not derive all of its components from a single theoretical base but rather takes its premises from elements of models which meet the empirical requirements derived from quality organizations.

In this sense TQM is very attractive to most

organizations because it is not culturally specific; it can evolve in response to the particular circumstances assuming that here is a supplier-customer relationship. Thus TQM is operating in Japan, the USA, Germany and Britain. It is operating successfully in giant car manufacturers, hospital accident and emergency units, charitable organizations, local government, etc. It would therefore seem possible that it might apply to schools and colleges. Although there are no detailed evaluations of TQM in education available there are some helpful parallels to draw on. Hopkins (1987) identifies a range of factors which characterize effective schools:

- curriculum-focused leadership,
- supportive climate,
- emphasis on learning,
- clear goals and high expectations,
- monitoring performance,
- continuous staff development,
- parental involvement,
- LEA support.

Fullan stresses the importance of process issues in developing effective schools, i.e. leadership as a process, consensual value systems, sophisticated social interactions and collaborative planning. The links between these approaches and the principles outlined in Figure are clear and would seem to reinforce the view that the principles of TQM are already available to schools, however implicitly.

However, there are a number of possible objections to TQM in the education service, especially schools and colleges:

(1) Professional autonomy - 'no person is an island but teachers come pretty close'. Teaching is often perceived of as an essentially solitary activity which therefore creates a high degree of individual control. Such an approach is clearly alien to the co-operative ethos of TQM. However, serious questions have to be raised as to the validity of this approach. The twinned requirements of the self-governing school and the national curriculum argue against the validity of the individualistic approach. Schools are increasingly having to respond as organizations and the management of the national curriculum requires high level of integration and collaboration whilst preserving team and personal discretion.

(2) Managerialism - 'management is about conformity, education is about preparing the individual to live in a democratic society'. This view argues that education and management are inimical. As has been argued above, TQM is a process which derives its content and values from the needs of its clients. Thus TQM in a company producing luxury cars will be driven by consumerism - ion a Scholl it needs to be driven by educational values. Indeed it could well be argued that the respect for the individual central to TQM is preferable to the reactive, *ad hoc*, routinized administration that passes for management in some educational institutions.

(3) The customer - there has always been a problem in defining whom education is for, the child? the parent? the taxpayer? the State? The TQM response is to accept all claim to client status. It

is the process that defines the customer and accountability and not a debate between alternative value systems. Thus the child is the customer in the classroom, the parent is the customer for reporting procedures, the LEA, DES and HMI are equally customers i context. One of the problematic in applying TQM to education is how potential tensions between these customers might be reconciled.

(4) Problematic outcomes - if education is viewed as a liberal, humanizing, long-term and heuristic process then an objective-driven approach such as TQM seems alien. However, it could be argued that the educated person is as tangible a concept as the satisfied customer or the healthy patient. Ends are elusive but it is possible to identify specific processes and activities that contribute to the outcome. It is these that are managed. Creating a love of literature may be problematic but specifying texts to be read, in what sequence, what learning methods are appropriate, how to assess progress, etc., can all be planned, measured and reviewed.

Total Quality Management is as yet relatively untried in the public sector in Britain; in the USA it is increasingly a norm. A great deal of empirical work is necessary to understand just how relevant the approach is to schools and colleges. However, it does offer a systematic, holistic and value-driven approach which has the potential to be developed. The most cogent argument for adopting TQM is the extent to which existing practices are felt to be appropriate and successful for schools and colleges in an era of increasing institutional autonomy.

11 The Management of Time

While headteachers are not required to become experts in accountancy, marketing, law and so on, the range of their responsibilities, nevertheless, has widened. If senior staff are to continue to exercise academic leadership in addition to these new responsibilities then the management of time becomes a crucial issue on their agenda. The limitation of finite amount of time is identified by many headteachers as one of the most serious constraints they face in attempting to meet the challenges presented by the changed managerial arena.

Images have been used to attempt to capture the nature of time. It has been presented as a commodity with a currency value which may vary in exchange rate according to social geographic or market forces. In some cultures one is made to feel guilty if time is 'wasted' while in others time is regarded more casually. Benjamin Franklin took the imagery a stage further when he counselled 'remember that time is money': time is certainly now accounted in terms of sums of money per hour, per week, per month, per year. The increasing use in education of techniques like cost - benefits analysis implies a management to school level will require those who have managerial responsibility to engage in this kind of accounting exercise. Managers in schools are often surprised to discover that a staff meeting of fifty members of staff meeting of fifty members of staff for three hours at a nominal eight pounds per hour for each participant costs one thousand two hundred pounds. This puts a premium on the worthwhile utilization of time.

Time may also be seen as the composite total of that available to and utilized by all the staff in the school. The stipulation under the School Teachers' Pay and Conditions Order of a minimum of 1,265 hours has made teachers particularly sensitive to the extent of their obligation in terms of time. Headteachers, therefore, have had to look at the total deployment of staff time and to agree with individual members of staff how their time is to be used. Clear job specifications for staff, negotiated through sympathetic and reciprocal processes of appraisal which relate to the aims and objectives of the school and the priorities identified, can be useful instruments in achieving more effective utilization of the total bank of time available. However, the dangers of teachers' contracts which are tightly defined may be seen in many American schools where principals find it impossible to hold meetings after school hours or to persuade staff to engage in extra-curricular activities. This chill wind is already being felt in the United Kingdom and can only be avoided by the establishment of sensitive relationships which allow flexibility.

In many of the devolved activities of LMS there

will be a need for effective staff development if delegated tasks and functions are to be undertaken successfully. Such initiatives will demand valuable time and sympathetic provision by LEAs. For example, in many primary schools where curriculum development has been growing in volume and more closely associated with the new allowance structures, staff have been relating uneasily to unfamiliar roles. In such times of significant change and insecurity LEAs must be generous in providing opportunity for development and regeneration. It is important to build solid foundations for future evolution. Advisory and consultancy services working in partnership with institutions of higher education can offer invaluable support and guidance. Schools can also look at different sources of provision and buy appropriately, having made a searching diagnosis of needs and priorities. Educational institutions will have to learn, like many successful private sector organizations, that ongoing staff development is of key importance and costs money and time.

More responsibilities deriving from the schools will demand more time. Local financial management is a key example. Decision making structures will be required to determine financial priorities before arriving at the activities of budgeting and accounting. There has been a movement towards more participation in decision making at middle-management level and below but such democratic involvement consumes time. However, it need not be time taken up wholly in meetings. Staff can be encouraged to submit ideas and proposals in written form which may be considered by senior management and the problematic areas addressed specifically.

The other side of the coin is the removal of layers of intermediate administration which inhibit the school's ability to act swiftly. In the past schools wishing to purchase items of equipment had to approach a purchasing officer in the LEA who followed a lengthy procedure of obtaining estimates and choosing an appropriate provider. While the headteacher is accountable to the school governors for good housekeeping and must spend wisely, it will now be possible to expedite purchase. Admission of pupils to schools, which is considered in the second chapter of the 1988 Act, offers another example of time saving to hard-pressed management. No longer do schools have to await the LEA decision on admission numbers arrived at in arbitrary fashion and often too late for effective decision making. Open enrolment may be threatening to many schools but it will certainly save time.

Identifying priorities

Approaches to more effective management of time have often taken as a starting point the compilation of a diary chronicling how time is utilized at present. This approach is predicated on a belief prevalent in management literature that it is important to know where you are now before determining where you want to go. The problem with this method of attack is the difficulty in designing an analytic instrument which makes sense of the myriad of data obtained. The result is that many investigations such as that undertaken by Hall, Mackay, and Morgan simply reflect what headteachers in schools already know - that their working day is hectic and fragmented and their activity characterized by brevity and variety. The approach proposed here is to identify priorities in the use of time as a first step so that the process of analysis and evaluation which follows is more clearly focussed within an appropriate framework.

Establishment of priorities and goals is a key activity for the effective education manager otherwise s(h)he is likely to be blown by whatever wind is strongest. In the nebulous world of education, where ends and means are questioned and disputed, the lack of clarity is often compounded by the manager who takes on everything that is asked of him or her and is unwilling to say 'No'. The setting of priorities is about deciding what is important and the following priorities profile is offered as an aid to such investigation.

Priorities profile

- *What are your long-term aspirations for the school?* A common problem claimed by staff in schools is that it is difficult to identify and sustain a clear sense of mission. The vision of the way forward becomes lost in the clinging mud of day-to-day problems and emergencies.

- *What do you identify as your role in pursuing these aspirations?* It is important that senior management takes a helicopter view so that the urgent and pressing but less important does not force out consideration of important objectives both in the short-term and long-term. The headteacher, in particular, has a central responsibility to keep the main objectives of the school in sight.

- *What do you see as your major management priorities?* Koter maintains that it is crucial for the manager to have a clear 'agenda' with established priorities. He argues that, although the manager's world is frenetic, spasmodic, and often reactive, it is, nevertheless, purposive. For example, a deputy headteacher with responsibility for staff development may determine needs and exercise influence through the informal networks. The daily encounters with colleagues may provide opportunities to share and explore issues of concern both for the individual and the school.

- *What are the main management activities involved on pursuing these priorities*? It is important for senior staff to identify the main management tasks and to decide which to retain and which to delegate. The headteachers have considerable flexibility in determining what their major contributions are to be but must ensure that the various functions are clearly assigned. The headteachers retains ultimate accountability and the functions newly developed to school level must be included among the priorities.

By a carefully planned and clearly articulated process of delegation senior staff can have a more certain picture of the specific activities each wishes or is required to be engaged in. For example,within the new framework of the national curriculum a senior teacher may have curriculum design as a high priority. It will be necessary to look beyond the 'global curriculum' and to identify key areas for attention. Such areas may be determined by the core and foundation subjects of the proposed national curriculum or it may be expedient to respond to growing and newly developing areas like economic awareness, health education, and information technology. In both cases it is necessary to decide the nature of the support to be given, the action required and the demands on energy and time.

Primary schools will have particular difficulty in finding time for curriculum development and in addressing the many activities associated with LMS. As primary teachers tend to relate to one class or grouping for most of the working day it is not easy to find cover to release staff. This is also particularly true of the teaching principal in smaller schools. Some schools have met this challenge by adopting pedagogical approaches like team teaching and resource-based learning. Other primary schools have formed cluster group or consortia to allow exchange of staff and, in some cases, an extra member of staff has been negotiated with the LEA to manufacture free time and to obtain specialist curriculum expertise.The challenge is to look closely and critically at prevailing practice and to devise ways of making time available.

Present USE of time

The following questions should assist the manager to compile a more complete picture of present management activities and to compare these with the desired activities identified through the use of the priorities profile paying particular attention to the new demands imposed by the 1988 Act.

(1) What are the main management activities in which you engage at present?

(2) How are these activities determined? (job description, prescription from above, negotiation, established practice, self-determination.)

(3) Are these the activities identified as your priorities?

(4) How much time do you give to important and less important tasks as you see them?

(5) How much time do you spend on activities which you feel do not benefit pupils, staff, the school or yourself ? On whom/what is this time spent?

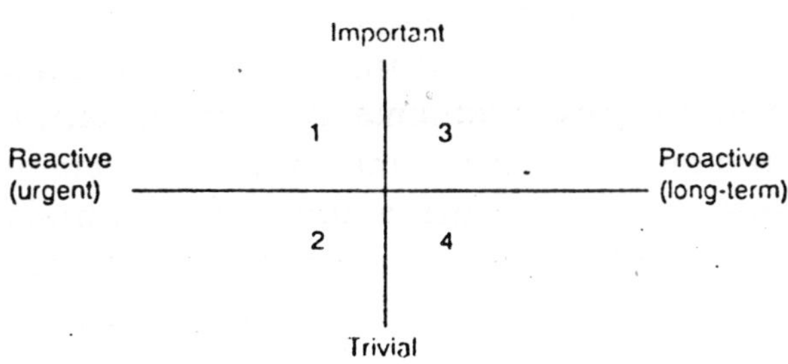

Classification framework

A searching, rigorous response to the above questions requires some kind of methodical investigation of present practice.The priorities identified and ordered earlier and the nature of the specific questions to which an answer is desired will determine the choice of approach used to ascertain how time is currently spent. It is desirable for the individual to design a specific instrument on the basis of the priorities identified. Too often instruments are designed without a clear perception of the exact information that is required and in what form it is wanted.

It is likely that most managers operate in quadrants 1 and 2 and are therefore working under constant stress and pressure. Often they may not be initiating events but are merely reacting to demands from others. Perhaps they are unwilling to say 'No' and therefore are doing many of the tasks which should be done by colleagues. There may be a lack of clarity about role and functions in the school so that unexpected problems are more likely to surface. Quadrant 2 is perhaps the most uncomfortable and least satisfying in which to reside although some managers may be happy to feel busy engaging in trivial pursuits. A manager in quadrant 3 is more likely to be undertaking important tasks and addressing key problems in circumstances over which s(he) has control and influence. Hopefully the message is clear - routine and trivial administrative tasks and crisis action are categories of activity that should be reduced and replaced as far as possible by the important, whether immediate or long-term. Perhaps one of the positive outcomes of the 1988 Act will be to encourage schools and their governing bodies to engage in more proactive long-term activities and in this context the issue of strategic planning addressed later in this chapter is of particular importance.

Self-evaluation

The scrutiny of how time is utilized leads inevitably to scrutiny of self. It is only by knowing ourselves better that many of the difficulties and resolutions may be identified. Often we are inclined to step back and refuse to acknowledge certain aspects of our personality which pose problems. Appropriate excuses are often made: 'I always work best under pressure'; 'I cannot respond until I have the necessary information to hand'; 'If colleagues have problems I cannot refuse to see them'; 'It will not be done if I do not do it myself'. An honest response to the following self-evaluation profile will provide helpful indicators of temperament and disposition, strengths and weaknesses. It also asks about activity which is not work related but makes an important contribution to a more complete, balanced, and fulfilled life.

Self-evaluation profile

- Which management activities do you do best?
- Which management activities do you dislike doing?
- When and in what circumstances do you feel under time pressure?
- Do you feel that you succeed in balancing work-based activities and your private life? If not, which areas are neglected?
- Do you feel that generally you have energy and dynamism to spare?
- Do you manage to build free time into your working day?
- If you could remodel your job what changes would you make?
- If you could recorder your allocation of time what changes would you make?

The answers to the above questions should increase self-awareness and identify some of the time problems that managers typically encounter. Often managers will choose to do things which they like or which they can do well. Where there is lack of competence or tasks are disagreeable and difficult then these are likely to be left undone. This has implications for self-development and staff development in the school. The self-evaluation profile can be used to identify interests, strengths and weaknesses of senior members of staff. However, it is likely that areas will be identified in which no member of staff appears to have a particular interest or expertise. Nevertheless, these areas have to be attended to and competences have to be developed so that all aspects of the management task are accomplished. [...] As stated earlier the headteacher does not have to become an accountant but often expertise does reside at a senior level within the school. Ideally there is a case for an ancillary addition to establishment with expertise and seniority.

Research into educational institutions has indicated that early morning is often the busiest time - telephone calls, correspondence, unresolved problems from the previous day are typical pressures on the manager. Schools are also characterized by cyclical activity. Budgeting, requisitioning, timetabling, and the preparing of reports and profiles are characteristic examples and may be alleviated by appropriate delegation and dispersion. It is likely that the reader can identify colleagues who are 'workaholics'. Typically they work long hours and bring reams of paper home. Family, friends and leisure suffer at the expense of work. Adam points out that the Pareto principle also applies to time - 80 per cent of the really productive, creative work will be done in 20 per cent of the time. Allocation of appropriate time to home, family, relaxation, and recreation will lead to a happier, more fulfilled, balanced life style and reduce the likelihood of stress-related illnesses. Research has indicated that managerial activity is often fragmented, unremitting, and spontaneous. Much of this piecemeal, disjointed behaviour may be positive and purposive but equally much may occur because of lack of organization and the assumption of an unthinking management style.

Obstacles to effective time management

The last two questions in the evaluation profile ask managers to look critically at their present activity and allocation of time and to devise ways in which both may be revised to increase effectiveness. Such diagnosis may be helped by the identification of recurring problems in managing time which may be tackled and overcome.

Procrastination

To defer or put off action until some future time without reasonable justification is a very human failing. Compelling reasons may be sought and produced: 'I'm too busy now to respond to that problem - I'll look at it again when I have more time' or 'Allow the dust to settle'. It may be on occasion that deferment is a sound course of action but if it happens habitually then its validity must be questioned. Often unpleasant or demanding tasks are put off which become more difficult with each succeeding day. In addition, work piles up and important information may be buried with it leading to missed deadlines. If it has become habitual to be dilatory then one must determine to break the pattern. Often it is a case of taking a simple, first step-that meeting with the awkward member of staff or breaking of unwelcome news - which often turns out to be less threatening than was imagined.

It is perhaps more difficult to change behaviour which reflects a casual and easy-going personality. The setting of personal deadlines and adhering to them offers one way of establishing order and priority. It is salutary to remember that tomorrow never comes and the temptation to defer should be resisted.

Open door

'Open door' became a fashionable management maxim in the 1960s. It suggested management which was accessible, responsible and sympathetic but for many managers the other side of the coin was a plethora of often unwelcome interruptions. Clearly it is important to offer ready access to staff, parents, or other parties if the need arises and in such circumstances interruptions may be inevitable. However there are valid and invalid interruptions, and judgements have to be made to decide the validity of claims on time. There are a number of filters which may be employed. If structures and channels of communication are clearly delineated the caller may be referred to the pertinent member of staff. Very often headteachers and senior managers have a secretary or access to one who can defer callers, keep them at bay or pass them to the appropriate colleague. This has implications for effective delegation which will be considered later. When the enforced interruptions are inevitable there are strategies which may be employed to abbreviate them:

- Identify the purpose of the visit and stick to it.
- Set apart times of the day for open access.
- Limit the time for each caller and specify it.

- Body language is important: do not become comfortably seated and established.

Task jumping

Often the most frequent source of interruption is the manager him(her)self. If a task becomes difficult then one is tempted to turn to something else. Many find it difficult to concentrate for protracted periods of time. It is prudent to remember that more is likely to be achieved in one hour of continuous application than in several hours of interrupted work because a recovery period is necessary after each stoppage. It is expedient to discover if the task jumping is self-inflicted. Mintzberg found that five chief executives under investigation 'frequently interrupted their desk work to place telephone calls or to request that subordinates come by'. Martin and Willower in their investigation of the managerial behaviour of five high-school principals found that most of the activities that the subjects entered into ranged from one to four minutes and the modal time duration for the 3,730 tasks observed over 25 days was one minute. Also 50 per cent of all observed activities were interrupted. They call this pattern of behaviour 'The busy person syndrome'. Perhaps the sheer volume of work may offer some explanation but it would also appear that the managers contributed in part to the problem. Effort is required to break the frenetic cycle of activity and to build in some more coherent pattern of work.

Administrivia

In management terminology a distinction is often made in the United Kingdom between management and administration. Administration is portrayed as the mechanical, routine support and maintenance of a system with administrators frequently lacking the authority to make judgements and decisions in key areas like policy making and the allocation of resources. On the other hand, management involves crucial processes like problem solving, planning, decision making, organizing, leading, and influencing. The term 'administrivia' has a further connotation implying engagement in trivialities and unimportant detail. Hall, MacKay, and Morgan in their study of fifteen headteachers demonstrated that some devoted considerable time to such activity and it is certainly a common complaint by headteachers that 'administrivia' so often takes over. There are clear implications for judicious delegation and the sharing out of routine matters to allow senior management to address important matters of policy and its implementation.

Meetings

Hall, Mackay, and Morgan also discovered that an overwhelming volume of headteachers' activity was interpersonal. While many of the inter changes were with individuals, a considerable amount of time was taken up with meetings. A meeting may be described as the organized or spontaneous coming together of people at a common time and place for specific purposes. These purposes may be predetermined or may arise from a chance encounter with a group of colleagues. Because meetings may take up and waste substantial amounts of time headteachers have to consider them critically. They may decide to carry out a review of meetings in the school and,in particular, those which they attend. Relevant questions may include:

- Are the meetings (series of meetings) necessary?
- If they are necessary what is their purpose?
- How often do they take place?
- How many meetings are required?
- Do I need to attend? If the answer is 'yes', do I need to attend all of them?

There is no doubt that meetings contribute vitally to the effective management of a school but it is to be suspected that many unnecessary meetings are held when the group has already fulfilled or when intervening activity or time for reflection is required. Meetings may serve a variety of purposes including the following:

- Information giving/exchange
- Direction
- Problem solving
- Discussion
- Negotiation
- Decision-making

It may well be that many of these activities occur in the course of a meeting but it is helpful for the manager to have a clear, predominant purpose in mind. Because meetings are costly as illustrated earlier, the manager may decide to be ruthless on their review.

However, in a dynamic school,meetings are important instruments which encourage commitment and participation and if they are necessary then there are ways of saving time. It may be appropriate to delegate functions to smaller groups who report back either to senior management,larger groupings,or full staff meetings. It is worthwhile to prepare carefully and to provide preliminary documentation which may be digested before rather than during the meeting. If possible formal meetings should not be called at short notice. Agenda should be brief and adhered to.

The chairperson occupies a key position in acting both as leader and adjudicator. The chairperson can decide in advance what is the maximum time for each item and, if necessary, operate a guillotine. The tone of the meeting may be set by a clear exposition of the purpose of the meeting and by demonstrating conciseness and clarity throughout. It is sound practice not to allow decisions arrived at in previous meetings to be reconsidered and reversed unless there are serious reasons for so doing. The chairperson can discourage the discursive, dominant, and dilatory and be firm, fair and supportive without being dismissive. The momentum should be sustained without losing healthy, pertinent discussion and the generation of ideas.

Strategies for more effective time management

Having identified some of the problems which may contribute to time pressure for those who manage schools some strategies for recovery, if not total cure, emerge from the process of diagnosis.

Planning and the setting of goals

Many experts who have pronounced and written on management, stress the importance of setting goals or intentions for the organization and by implication for those who work within it. This projection of targets, a looking and thinking forward in time, is central to the process of planning. While recognizing the political and transitory reality of schools it is nevertheless possible by careful, proactive planning to make more effective use of time. The term 'goal' clearly derives from sporting endeavors and is the declared intention of teams of players. There is the implication that all team members are or should be co-operating and contributing to that end. Such a claim should not be taken for granted in organizations like schools where territory and competition are central to the culture and value systems, and may stimulate behaviour which does not seek to pursue common aims. Equally status, reward, autonomy, professional interest and individual fulfilment are personal goals which may not be in harmony with the goals of those who manage and therefore seek the general good of the school.

The activities of review and audit seek to offer a more complete picture of the working environment. Review reminds us that knowing where we have been (the past) and where we are (the present) are vital contributions to determining where we want to go (the future). The activity of audit identifies what opportunities and threats are facing the school and what are strengths and weaknesses. This exercise reminds us that managing is the art of the possible and the process of audit is about deciding what is possible.

Mission has become a popular term in planning parlance and refers to the overall aspirations of the school. The mission statement may be regarded as

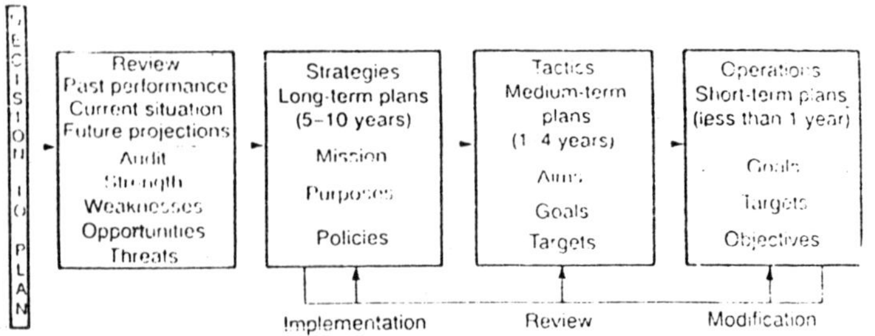

The planning process

the foundation stone of school purposes and policy. The terms 'aim' and 'goal' are often used interchangeably and express in general terms intentions which the school seeks to pursue. Targets and objectives are usually more specific declarations of intent often expressed in behavioural terms. It is sound practice to make aims, goals, and objectives as specific and realistic as possible and to ensure that they are attainable but demanding. It is also expedient to set reasonable deadlines which may be modified if circumstances change. By judicious management of time the headteacher can ensure that (s)he is properly engaged in the development of strategies and tactics rather than becoming total enmeshed in short-term operations.

Delegation

There is, in typical school, an often untapped bank of expertise and knowledge available from both staff and pupils. Frequently senior managers are tempted to undertake tasks which can be carried out very competently by others. the delegation of such tasks should free the manager to engage in higher order management activities like planning, policy making, and innovating. Management arena also indicates priorities which will be high on the agenda of schools in the near future. Banking offers the term 'audit' to management vocabulary to indicate that talent and competence can be identified. Staff may be encouraged to specify their strengths by means of a sensitively administered questionnaire or through skillful appraisal techniques. The utilization of those strengths offers a rich source of fulfilment and motivation at a time when a lack of mobility both within and between schools is likely to lead to debilitation and declining morale. Delegation should also be an important tool of staff development and it should not be seen as an opportunity for passing the unpleasant, boring aspects of management to other staff. Joa Dean offers a useful questionnaire: if the manager responds affirmatively to statements about working long hours, concentrating on minutiae, carrying out jobs which could be done by others and believing that the manager can do most jobs better than colleagues then it is likely that there is not enough delegation.

The simple model in Figure illustrates the delegation process. The principle of parity indicates that the process of delegation involves giving the subordinate sufficient authority to carry out a decision as well as responsibility for it. In the education system ultimate accountability resides with the headteacher although authority and responsibility may be delegated. However, it may be difficult for staff who are relatively junior in the school to exercise authority over senior management or, on occasion, middle management such as heads of department and year heads. This may necessitate political skills such as negotiation, bargaining, persuasion and compromise. One has also to remember that professional teachers are likely to resists bureaucratic control as typified in the terms 'boss' and 'subordinate'. It may be more acceptable for the superior to present themselves as a co-ordinator, facilitator or enabler managing a team of professional specialists.

- Effective delegation may consist of the following activities:
- Find out the competences and experience of intended delegates.
- Introduce intention and ascertain willingness.
- Organize relevant staff development activity.
- Define parameters and outcomes of task and allocated resources.
- Check understanding and agreement
- Determine procedures and structures which may be followed if problems arise: delegation is not abdication.
- Provide for contingencies.
- Grant and make public the necessary authority over staff and resources.
- Offer feedback and positive reinforcement where appropriate.
- Carry out regular review unobtrusively.

Peak time

There are differences between individuals in relation to when they work best. Some maintain that they work most effectively late at night while others prefer to rise early and use the first hours of the morning. Physiologists claim that the human metabolism is governed by biorhythms or cycles which are reinforced by the imposed periods of sleep and waking. This would suggest that people should be fresher and more energetic in the morning after a good night's rest. Given that the human body also burns energy through the course of a hard working; day it is likely that teachers who have worked hard from early morning to the end of the school day may find it difficult to regenerate themselves to reasonable levels of efficiency in the evening. The argument to date supports the validity of testing one's capacity to work in the early morning if this has not been tried before or at least to use the morning hours in preference to afternoon or evening. Research also indicates that people work better if there are breaks to allow the systems to revitalize itself. The number and timing of breaks may be determined by the nature of the task being undertaken. Creative work demands freshness and dynamism while routine administration may be less demanding. Nevertheless, repetitive work also demands concentration if mistakes are to be avoided.

Psychologists claim that the mind works even during sleep and in the process of sleeping on a problem the subconscious mind may offer a solution. Apart from the possibility of new insights it also makes sense to 'sleep' on an important decision to avoid arriving at unwarranted conclusions in the heat of the moment. Adair offers the concept of 'moonlighting' which he describes as waking naturally in the early hours of the morning with ideas should be recorded and captured. The danger of saturation apportioning the school day if protracted concentration is required. such endeavor can be punctual by less demanding activities such as more informal conversations with staff or visitors.

Long working hours, excessive paper work, the pressure of deadlines, frequent interruptions, and the intrusion of the unexpected all contribute to a working environment which offers no opportunity to recharge batteries or to pause for reflection and critical review f what the school is doing and where it is going. Unremitting pressure of work is likely to lead to stress and the myriad of accompanying symptoms which are often recognized only at crisis point. Perhaps the increasing inclusion of consideration of stress in conference sessions and the growing volume of research into its causes and remedies are indications of a growing recognition of pressures in schools, not least the pressure of time. If the manager can set apart a period of time each day for quiet reflection and consideration of what tomorrow and the longer term future may bring, it is more probable that s(h) can remain in control of the management environment. The time log mentioned earlier offers an instrument to review critically what is being done. The manager can ask two questions: 'Is this activity necessary?', and 'What would happen if I did not do it?' Delegation and the reduction of time spent in attending meetings and routine administration may offer the opportunity to do less a little better and to make that small but vital oasis of free time for regeneration and relaxation. Colleagues and secretaries may be conditioned to respect and protect it and the location of the daily half an hour may alter from day to day to accommodate the changing pattern of management practice.

12 Developing Quality in Education

What is meant by quality?

There are a number of overlapping perspectives - drawn from industry and commerce - which seek to define the meaning of quality. Each perspective has a rather different emphasis. Quality may be about perfection, inspection, conformance to requirements, fitness for purpose, improving customer/client satisfaction, or empowering the customer/client. These perspective raise interesting implications when applied to education. Does inspection - the ritual pouring on of quality at the end of a process - mean that 20% of student must fail in order to "preserve standards"? Does conformance to requirements - which emphasises "quality systems" and "getting it right first time", prevention rather than inspection - reduce a teacher's freedom to abandon a well-planned class and attend to a particular concern or difficulty? Does fitness for purpose beg the empowering the customer/client - giving power to the student - mean enhancing their ability to exact sanctions if they think that the education they have received is unsatisfactory?

In the opinion of the author, quality is about

improving customer/client satisfaction .or, in educational terms, improving the quality of learning for students. In practice, this means engaging in a systematic and continuous process of development and incremental change that is heavily dependent for its success on all the "partners" having meaning, purpose and satisfaction in their work.

Where can quality be developed?

A very simple model of a school can be constructed which identifies the major processes policies, staff, students, resources, and so forth. Transformations include teaching, tutoring, learning, assessing, as well as staff training and development. Outcomes include the academic, personal and social development of students and staff, and examination results. The satisfaction of students, their parents, their future employers, and so froth, with the education that has been provided should also be considered. It is clear that to develop quality in all these aspects of a school's work would be a formidable and in some respects perhaps an unnecessary task: priorities for development must be established. This issue has been well recognised in schools with the introduction of school development plans. Such plans identify specific objectives to be achieved during the forth coming year and include detailed action plans to show how these are to be achieved, and longer term objectives for the following two or three years. Staff appraisal schemes are now being introduced in schools and will help to ensure that the need and aspirations of individual teachers are in harmony with the needs and aspirations of the school, as articulated in the school development plan.

How can quality be developed?

Wale and Ribbins have led a major initiative in quality development in the Brimingham LEA. They have brought together the experience schools have acquired in development planning with a systematic approach to monitoring and evaluating. Building on their work, the author has emphasised the importance of considering the present and future needs of the stakeholders or partners in the school, of systematic strategy for implementing planned change, and of leadership and team work. Thus developing quality in education is, in the author's opinion, a systematic and continuous process that involves four core elements: strategic and action planning; implementing, monitoring and evaluating planned change; responsive and flexible leadership; and co-operative and supportive team work. These four core elements are clearly related to Oakland's four major components of total quality management: a quality system; statistical process control; management commitment; and team work. The author has found Oakland's ideas and analysis invaluable. The following quotation, in particular, has proved most useful when talking to colleagues about total quality management.

"The author and his colleagues have heard the excuse that "our industry (or organization) is different to any other industry (or organization)' in almost every industry or organization with which they have been involved. Clearly, there are technological differences between all industries and nearly all organizations, but in terms of managing total quality there are hardly any at all"

A course for quality development

The course was a three-term, ninety-hour course for experienced teachers in primary and secondary schools leading to an Advanced Certificate in Education or, with further study, at MEd. The first two terms' work consisted of lectures, discussions and workshops, and tutorial support for the assignments. The third term's work was devoted to action learning projects which focused on quality development in the teacher's own schools. The course was held not at the University but, on alternative weeks, at two of the teachers' schools outreach centres. The author's aim statement for the curse was:

"To design and deliver a course - based on the four core elements; planning feedback leadership; and team work - that will enable the participants to develop the knowledge, skill, experience, confidence and enthusiasm to begin and to continue the work of quality development in their own schools."

The course was built around ten key questions. The first four of these focused on strategic planning: What are we here for? Where are we now? Where do we want to get to? What do we need to focus on? Thinking about the second and third of these questions naturally leads to the fourth: the "quality gap". The fifth question was about action planning: How do we get there?

A systematic strategy for implementing planned change was described in response to the sixth question: How do we effect change? This strategy involved identifying the various stakeholders who were effecting or were affected by the change, and then analysing each group in terms of six decisive factors. these are; linkage; openness; gain/loss; ownership; leadership; and power. The different purposes for monitoring an evaluating and the different techniques—questionnaires, interviews, and observation schedules—were also described to answer the seventh the eight questions: How are we doing? How have we done?

The following Oakland's suggestions, some numerical performance indicators were also collected for each term's module of the course. For example, the average percentage attendance; the percentage of assignments handed in for marking; the medians of the students' response to an end-of-term questionnaire: the percentage of students who continued on to the following term. This data was, arguably, invaluable for monitoring the quality of the course and to demonstrate that the author "practiced what he preached". It does not explain the reasons for problems but certainly shows if problems exist. Such data has not been commonly collated in School of Education but as an increasing amount of our work takes place in outreach centres or is on contract, it will be needed to fulfill any requirements for accountability. When similar data becomes available it will be very interesting to compare the performance of the course at all four outreach centres, and indeed with more traditional curses that are held in the School of Education.

In practice, these eight questions or stages in planning for quality development fuse into one another. And the process of planning is at least as important as the final document. However, ensuring that the plan is actually implemented, monitored and evaluated - which depends on leadership and team work - are the most difficult and challenging parts of the whole process. Thus the last two questions in the course focused on leadership and team work: How can we develop our effectiveness as leaders? How can we build teams?

A number of perspectives on leadership and team building proved useful in the course. First, there are the personal qualities and associated actions that followers look for in leaders if they are to give exceptional performance. Kouzes and Posner identify your such qualities: honesty; competence vision and enthusiasm. they emphasise that credibility is the foundation of leadership. Second, there is the work of Adair which focuses on three complementary functions that the effective leader must attend to: achieving the task; building the team; and developing the individuals in the team. Adair and Belbin have much to say about building teams that the course members appreciated. Third, there is the work of Blanchard et al which emphasises that followers have different needs, which depend on the particular task in hand, so that the leaders need a variety of styles and the ability to match the appropriate style to the followers' needs. Fourth, the work of Argyris and Schon on theory-of-action underlines the difficulty of practising what we preach, of ensuring that our behaviour really does match our stated values.

13 Quality of Assessment

Much of this volume is about the assessment of quality—this paper is about the quality of assessment. What our students really pay for are then degrees or their diplomas or their certificates. Yet we put much more emphasis in trying to teach our students than we normally put into designing assessment - particularly the "formal assessment" that counts towards final qualifications. Assessment is where learners often get a raw deal.

The 1991 AETT conference had the theme "Developing And Measuring Competence" As one of the editors of the proceedings of that conference, I became well acquainted with the many views on competence which were aired by the various contributors. It was heartening to see that many of the approaches to the development of competence focused on defining the evidence which would be sufficient to demonstrate competence.

However, I was left with some concerns about whether competence would often end up as minimum competence rather than high competence. Some questions about "shades" of competence, and about a range of descriptors which may be needed to provide more information than simply "can do".

Higher education in the United Kingdom is being moved steadily towards greater participation rates. This move includes not only rapidly increasing numbers of school leavers, but also many more non-traditional entrants. Everywhere, lecturers and tutors are seeking help in handling large classes. It is clear that the workload of staff in higher education is increasing, as they become responsible for more and more learners.

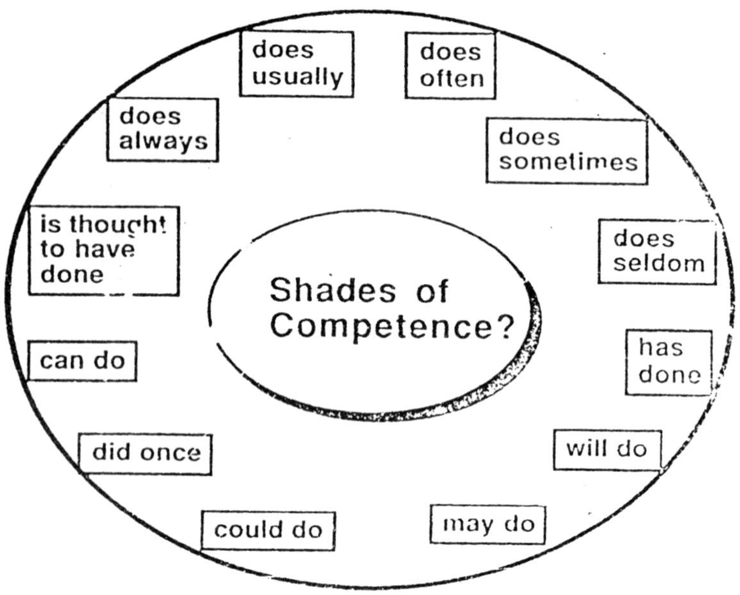

Shades of competence

In some ways, teaching can be "done to" large numbers almost as easily as to small numbers - it's almost as easy to lecture to 300 as to lecture to 100. However, teaching greater numbers may have little connection with learning by greater numbers. And when it comes to assessment, there are no short cuts. It usually takes three times the amount of time to assess 300 learners as it would to assess 100 learners. The main challenge we face as we move towards a mass higher education system, is merely maintaining the quality of assessment we presently have - not to mention improving it.

How most people learn

First, consider how people learn - real people, that is, not educational psychologists or their learners! During the last couple of years, I've given thousands of people post-its, and asked them to write down the answers to the following questions on them.

1. Think of something you're good at - something you do well. Write down a few words about how you became good at it.
2. Think of something you *feel* good about - something that gives you a "glow". Write down a few words explaining your *evidence* for this good feeling.
3. Think of a learning experience that was not successful. Write down a few words explaining what went wrong.

The answers to "I" are almost always along the following lines:

- doing it
- practice
- trial and error
- learning from mistakes.

In other words, most people learn by doing

rather than by sitting at the feet of masters or mistresses.

The answers to "2" are usually along the following lines:

- feedback from others
- other people's reactions
- because I can see the effect.

In other words, to feel good about something, people need feedback. The answers to "3" are more complex. Sometimes they reflect things that went wrong with the "learning by doing" stage—for example lack of opportunity to practice. Sometimes they reflect things that went wrong with the feedback stage—in other words lack of the opportunity to develop good *feelings* about what had been learned. Two more problems often emerge:

- lack of motivation in the first place
- lack of opportunity to make sense of the learning experience.

Linking traditional assessment to learning

So how does assessment usually relate to the four fundamental steps in the learning process? Let's take the most common form of assessment—the written examination.

- Wanting to learn (motivation)
- Not many people like exams! The fact that there is an exam coming along at the end of the road is not the strongest motivator for most people. The inevitability of traditional forms of

assessment is a key factor in preventing many people from participating in learning.

- Learning by doing (practice, learning from mistakes, and so on)

  Learning by doing can indeed happen during assessments, including written exams. Learning by doing can indeed happen during assessments, including written exams. Mistakes are indeed made during assessment - plenty of them! But learning by doing *while being assessed* is hardly the best way of using experiential learning. Besides, it is usually presumed that the learning should have taken place *before* the assessment event.

- Learning through feedback (to develop positive feelings about the learning) All assessment results in some sort of feedback. However, it's often the absolute minimum of feedback—for example a mere score—and that's weeks or months after the event! There is little or no real feedback, and chances to learn from the feedback are minimal.

- Digesting exams are better known for producing indigestion than for allowing people the chance to consolidate their learning. As I've said, the feedback is usually very limited in scope (and often delayed in time) and is not a useful means towards "digesting". Such feedback as there is, tends to be one way feedback. There's or no little chance to discuss the details or negotiate what best to do next.

At each step, assessment processes are at cross purposes with learning processes. Perhaps traditional forms of assessment have only one real contribution towards learning people are frightened (shamed) into doing some learning so that they may minimise their chances of being shown to be "lacking". Much intensive learning is done just before exams - but most of it is of a superficial nature,and soon forgotten again.

Ten worries - and some suggestions

I list below ten worries I have about assessment, outline my concerns, and offer some suggestions about how the problems may be minimised. Many of my suggestions point towards involving learners in their own assessment. This can be achieved by letting learners get their hands on the assessment criteria. It can be achieved even better by letting learners *apply* the assessment criteria, in self-assessment and peer-assessment. It is achieved best by helping learners to *formulate* the criteria, then apply them. An illustrated discussion of uses of self- and peer-assessment is included later in this paper.

1. Assessment is often done in a rush, to meet exam board deadlines. It's rarely done under the best of conditions!

This is because assessment tends to be done to learners - not by them. Assessment tends to be done at the end of learning something, rather than as a means to help the learning processes. In public exams, examiners often face piles of some hundreds of scripts, all of which need to be finished within only a week or two. Some suggestions for avoiding the problem are as follows:

- allow much more time for self assessment, so that it can be done well

- allow learners to use self-and peer-assessment, so they can learn by assessing.

2. Assessment is often done by bored people, tired of reading the same answers to the same questions (and seeing the same mistakes).

Examiners get thoroughly fed-up as they wade through hundreds of scripts. They get discouraged when they see things they hoped their learners would have mastered, only to find that messages have not got across. Any tedious or repetitive task causes people to change their mood. If assessors' moods plunge, the objectivity of assessment is likely to be affected accordingly.

- decrease the emphasis on traditional written exams altogether
- allow learners to learn by reading their own mistakes, and those of their peers.

3. Assessment tends to be governed by "what is easy to assess". Therefore, traditional written exams (relatively straightforward to assess) are used. These measure learners' skills at tackling traditional written exams.

There is still not enough attention being paid to what should constitute the evidence upon which to base awards. Many important competence are simply not assessable by traditional methods. While it is perfectly possible to use traditional methods to measure recall of facts and information, it is not-at-all easy to use such methods to measure innovation, judgement, or personality.

- look carefully at what is being measured by each form of assessment

- ·efrain from measuring the same things all the time -especially recall (people who can find and apply information are usually more valuable than people who simply happen to remember a lot of it)

4. Learners rarely know the intimate details of the assessment criteria, and how we interpret them.

There really is no excuse for this. The reason may be sinister - that those who design the assessment criteria are not sufficiently confident about them to show them to the learners! Assessors often fear that learners may demand to know "why did I get 65% for this, when my friend got 75%?" Surely, they have every right to ask this sort of question - and to learn from the feedback they should be given by way of a response to the question.

5. How should we develop learners' unassessable qualities? Should we refrain from developing them because we can't measure them?

"Don't bother to learn anything, when you can't see how they can ask you about it at the end of the day": this is a perfectly rational view taken by learners, deciding what to learn and what not to learn.

- bring the unassessable qualities firmly onto the agenda; explain to learners why they're important, and work out with learners what kinds of evidence can be linked to these qualities, and how the demonstration of that evidence can be built in to assessment procedures.

6. Almost all assessment processes in common use foster learner competition rather than

collaboration. No wonder our educated people are so bad at working in teams.

Learners preparing for exams are often quite secretive about the work they do. No-one likes to be thought of as a "swot"! However, it's more sinister than this; we actually compound the competition by using norm-referenced assessment far too much. In other words, only a certain proportion of learners are allowed to receive "A" grades, or 1st-class honours degree classifications. Therefore, learners *are* in competition.

- use criterion-referenced assessment only - abolish the use of norm-referencing
- help learners to feel that they can help each other prepare to demonstrate their competence, without disadvantaging one another.

7. What competences are measured by assessment anyway? Are they "can do" competences? Or are they simply "did do, once" ghosts?

Exams tend to measure "did once" competences. At their worst, they still remember "knew once" competences rather than "did once"!

- increase the proportion of assessment schedules allocated to continuous assessment which measures "is doing" competences rather than "did once" ones.

8. If we were to introduce "Quality in Assessment BS5750A": what should the criteria look like? What evidence of competence should *assessors* demonstrate?

At present, it is automatically assumed that anyone appointed to a post involving teaching or lecturing is blessed with all the skills needed to design assessment schemes and implement fair assessment. People are appointed to teaching (and assessing) posts not on the basis of how well they can do either task, but often on the record of their own academic performance.

- assess the assessors - have a system of "licences" to assess, and police the system thoroughly
- increase the uses of self-assessment and peer-assessment, which depend for less on subjectivity of assessors, and allow far greater amounts of feedback to contribute towards successful learning experiences.

9. "If you can't measure it, it doesn't exist. If you can measure it, it isn't it". What should we be trying to measure?

It has been said that one of the main faults of our education and training systems is that we tend to teach people things that are already understood, instead of equipping them to understand new things. Assessment reflects this.

- use self - and peer-assessment as an inherent part of learning processes, with the emphasis on learning rather than assessment outcomes.

10. Where stops the buck? Whose fault is it that assessment is so artificial? HoD? Employers? Assessors? Validators? The Government? Yours? Mine?

If you imply that there is something suspect about people's abilities to assess, it is badly received! Assessment is something that is usually done privately rather than publicly, and people go to great lengths to ensure that they retain privacy. Is such privacy really needed mainly because of the "put down the number you first thought of" syndrome?

Learning trough assessing

In much of my discussion so far, I've been focusing on the dangers when assessment is "done to" people, and hinting at the benefits which can result when learners themselves are allowed to be intimately involved in their own—and each other's—assessment. Self-assessment, and peer-assessment may lack some of the precision of the best of "formal" assessment - where (some) assessors have a great deal of experience, and (sometimes) assess fairly and conscientiously. However, what may be lacked in terms of precision is more than compensated for by the benefits of deeper learning, which go hand in hand with the act of learners themselves assessing.

Close Encounters with Assessment Criteria

This is the crucial difference between formal assessment, self-assessment and peer-assessment. Learners find out a lot about any subject simply by applying assessment criteria to examples of work in that subject (whether the examples are self-generated, made by other learners or issued by a teacher). Previously, assessment criteria have seemed to learners to be the property of examiners. There has been a tendency for teachers to regard assessment criteria as quite private. For many years, I marked "O"- level and "A"-level scripts for two of England's public examination boards, and the marking schemes have been required to be sent to external examiners or moderators, the vital information in such schemes has seldom been shared with learners, and until recently hardly ever *applied* by learners themselves. Yet when learners get the chance to get their hands on assessment criteria, they seem to develop a thirst for the information they can derive from them - leading to much deeper learning.

Self-assessment and peer-assessment are not just self-testing

These forms of assessment when well-developed involve two processes:

- involving learners in identifying standards or criteria to apply to their work
- allowing learners to make judgements about the extent to which they have met these standards and criteria.

Assessment criteria: Black and white or shades of grey?

In subjects like maths, science and engineering, things are often either right or wrong - and it is relatively easy to devise assessment criteria for tests and exercises. However, even in subjects such as law or social studies, there are identifiable hallmarks of a good answer or an unsatisfactory answer to a question. Such hallmarks can be turned into checklists of a flexible kind, which enable the characteristics of good and less good answer to be compared and contrasted. Students can benefit by learning in the act of applying assessment criteria to their own work, and to each others 'work'.

Benefits to learners of close encounters with assessment criteria

Learners can quickly find out about incorrect assumptions they have been making. They are able to find out the answer to the question; "What am I expected to become able to do?" There are of course many more benefits, depending on *how* we involved learners in using assessment criteria including helping learners themselves to formulate the criteria (when this is possible or appropriate) - leading to the most obvious form of ownership of assessment.

Some examples of self- and peer-assessment mechanisms

Self assessment is not confined to the variety that is widely used in open and distance learning (though of course that is one powerful form of it). Self assessment processes can include any of the following:

- providing learners with assessment criteria and a marking scheme and allowing them to mark their own work
- as above, but then allowing learners the chance to compare their mark with that of a "professional" marker
- as above, but also giving learners feedback about the quality of their self assessment
- enabling individual learners to generate assessment criteria, and use them to assess their own work
- enabling a group of learners to generate assessment criteria, and so on
- allowing learners to use core criteria generated by a group, plus additional criteria specific to

their own pieces of work, with an agreed weighting

- groups of learners can be issued with criteria to apply to each others' work
- groups of learners could produce criteria and apply them to each others' work.

There are further combinations of these. There is also the additional matter of whether the grades or scores contribute in a formal way to the performance records of learners.

Eliciting assessment criteria from a group

- I have found that the following approach gives useful results for groups of 10.20 (where 'x' could be an essay or presentation or handout and so on).
- I ask learners to go to groups of 3 or 4, and discuss criteria.
- I ask the groups to make a list of criteria, and to prioritise them.
- I flipchart the most important criteria from each group, then the next most important, etc.
- I ask the whole group whether anything important is missing from the flipchart list.
- I tidy up the flipcharted items if necessary, and number them.
- I ask each learner to privately distribute (eg.20) "marks" among the criteria.
- I write each learner's "mark" alongside each criterion on the flipchart. Then I either average them out, or allow each learner to apply his/her

own weightings in the peer assessments to follow.

- Learners then go off to perform the task (individuals or groups).
- I then produce a grid with their criteria and weightings, ready for peer assessment.

An example

I helped a group of students from a foundation course in Science, Engineering and Technology to generate and priorities some simple criteria for a short presentation that each student was to give to the group. (The presentations were optional; the assessment for the "Learning Strategies" module of the course contained six equal elements, and students could choose which five they tried - in other words they could choose not to give the presentation if they really wished to). We agreed that anyone who had the courage to get up and start immediately deserved to "pass"-in other words they got the first 40 marks there and then.

Each student filled in a grid for each of the presentations he or she witnessed (and students additionally self-assessed their own using the same criteria). For various reasons, some students were only able to be present for half of the time involved, and one or two students participated as assessors, but did not wish to give presentations themselves. I my self worked as one of the assessors, and was relieved to find that in general, the marks I awarded each of the presentations were close to the average mark for that presentation.

Learners' ownership of assessment criteria

The sort of peer-assessment described above is suitable for tasks such as presentations, where many people can assess the same piece of evidence, and where scores can then be compared and discussed by the group. For individual tasks such as essays, reports, projects, dissertations and so on, it is likely that each piece of work will reflect slightly different criteria (or even very different criteria),and then it is often best to allow for some "agreed" criteria, and some "idiosyncratic" criteria so that each learner can exercise more ownership of the assessment criteria.

The most important outcome of involving learners in the formulation of self-assessment or peer-assessment criteria, is that learners address the task with criteria in their minds, and the quality of their work seems to be much higher than it may otherwise have been.

Throw away the numbers or grades?

I've often suggested to learners after a peer assessment exercise that the numbers or grades awarded (if not contributing to their overall assessment) were only a vehicle to help them do learning of a higher productivity. However, I've found they usually want to hang on to the numbers - good or bad. Perhaps this is evidence of the sort of ownership we're aiming for?

How well can students assess themselves, and each other?

In general, students are quite accurate in their assessing. I have found that when students are asked to "guess" their own performance scores just after completing an exam, around 90% of students "guess" within 5% of their actual scores. It is useful to identify the 10% who had an inaccurate perception of how they had done - they usually benefit from a discussion to probe the causes. Those 10% may be over anxious, and underestimate their achievements, or over-confident and over-estimate their achievements. When discrepancies in self-assessment occur, they are usually due to one of the following causes:

- there is some tendency for learners to over-rate themselves in areas to which they are new - this tends to happen with the weaker members of the group
- there is a tendency for some leaders to under-rate themselves in areas in which they are experienced - this tends to happen with the more-skilled members of the group.

Peer-assessment and self-assessment can be usefully combined. Peer-assessment can be conducted "blind" so that "arranged" scoring is avoided. If the peer-assessment mark or grade is equal to the corresponding self-assessment mark (e.g. within 5%) then the self-assessment marks go forward into the assessment system - possibly with a staff "scan" to ensure that fair play is in operation. (It is far quicker to scan a piece of work to check whether the assessment is fair, than it is to mark the work from scratch). When self - and peer-scores differ, negotiation or staff intervention may be necessary (but this happens surprisingly rarely in practice).

Self-assessment, peer-assessment and learning

Throughout this paper, I've advocated the benefits of helping learners become intimately involved in processes of assessing, and I've pointed to the hazards of traditional assessment procedures. To conclude, lets look once again at the four main processes of learning, and see how self-and peer-assessment link to them.

- Wanting to learn (motivation)
- Motivation can be improved by early success. Self-assessment in particular can be used with the comfort of privacy, and learners can gain confidence by finding that they are "doing alright" long before they need to prove so publicly or formally.
- Learning by doing (practice, learning from mistakes, and so on)
- There's no better way to find out about one's successes and failures than by finding them out for oneself - or having a peer help one do this, rather than an "authority figure" like a tutor or examiner. The very act of assessing is intrinsically "learning by doing" - it involves the application of criteria, decision-making, judgement, and reflection.
- Learning through feedback (to develop positive feelings about the learning)
- The showstopper of formal assessment has to be the dreadfully limited feedback that is the norm. Peer-assessment can allow for a great deal of feedback - far more than could ever be given by a tutor or assessor. In addition, the feedback

gained in peer-assessment is usually far less threatening than that from "professional" assessors.Indeed,peers will often argue and debate issues, further deepening the usefulness of the feedback exchanges they receive.

- Digesting (taking stock, making sense of the experience, and of the feedback) Both self-assessment can help learners make sense of their learning experiences - and of the feedback they gain. Furthermore, the time lag between the learning and the feedback can be much less than with traditional methods of assessment. Therefore, the feedback is much more actively received and the learning thereby enhanced.

Reflecting on Assessment

It can be argued that people who need a "tester" are inadequately prepared to be sent out into the world outside. Self-assessment and peer-assessment can both be an important part of the learning process. The learning experience resulting from such forms of assessment is more important than the result of the assessment. Self-assessment or peer-assessment do not necessarily have to lead to any "formal" (recorded) assessment The aim can be purely as a learning experience, with the "marks" simply part of the process through which that experience is facilitated.

Self-assessment and peer-assessment are skills, and become more reliable with practice Receiving feedback on the quality of these forms of assessment is vital if learners are to derive the maximum benefit from engaging in them.

Self-assessment and peer-assessment should be introduced early - for example during the first term rather than being left until the final year. Late in a course, students may see little point in embracing new ways of learning.

"Ownership" is the most crucial aspect of successful learning, and both self assessment and peer-assessment are closely connected to the development of ownership of learning.

Not all students warm to the "exposure" of self- or peer-assessment. They may begin their studies with expectations that they will be assessed by professional. "What's in it for me?" they naturally may ask. They need to be convinced that self- and peer-assessment have direct benefits for themselves, and do not represent an abdication from duties on the part of tutors. Some tutors however feel it is dangerous to "lose control" of assessment. If such tutors try to employ self- or peer-assessment, but constantly safeguard their right to step in "should things go wrong", the whole concept of such form of assessment is undermined.

So what about teaching? Admittedly, our students learn from us. But they probably learn more on their own, and they probably learn even more from each other. Much of their learning occurs in the immediate run-up to assessment of one kind or another - so the role of assessment is an important factor in the circumstances which accelerate learning. Therefore, perhaps our biggest contribution to our students' learning is directly associated with the quality of the assessment our students encounter - and has less than we'd like to think to do with our teaching activities. I believe there is a strong case for using self- and peer-assessment not primarily to asses, but as processes to enhance learning.

Finally, if and when we must resort to traditional, formal assessment, I believe that there is a great deal of room for improvement. The "ten worries" I expressed earlier may help to set an agenda for improving the quality of assessment. I end this paper with 6 recommendations.

14 The Research Agenda

Broadfoot and others outline two levels of issue - the macro level relating to whether the new assessment system is meeting the purposes assigned it, and the micro level relating no classroom issues of implementation. Both require attention. The macro level, they state, 'is more than equally matched insignificance by the more micro issues of the actual quality of any of the assessment information generated'. R. Murphy, responding to the National Curriculum assessment proposals, identified issues of classroom practice, curriculum coverage, use of results and the reductive effects of a system designed to produce 'simple' information. the tension between the levels on which the National Curriculum assessments operate is a problem for research, firstly in that it generates o many research questions to be addressed within the very rapid period of introduction of the new system, and secondly because attention to individual issues or to levels of issue may appear to legitimate rather than question decisions taken at other levels. For example, research findings which identify undue expenditure of teacher time in preparing and administrating SATs, is equally capable in itself of justifying either a reduction in the complexity of the tasks, or a greater reliance on teacher assessment. These decisions would represent very different interpretations of the evidence related to different views of the purpose of the National Curriculum assessment. This chapter gives an overview of the fields of research and evaluation in which the National Curriculum assessments are being developed and investigated, and the extent to which different levels of issue can be addressed within the constraints which operate.

The speed of introduction of the National Curriculum has been and continuous to be, a very important constraint upon research and evaluation. The Report by the National Foundation for Educational Research and Bishop Grosseteste College, commissioned by SEAC, acknowledged the problem in making its recommendations: 'At the time of writing, decisions about the 1992 Standard Assessment task have already been taken. Hence, there is restricted likelihood of detailed research having a meaningful impact upon policy in the short term.

The scale of change, affecting all maintained schools in England and Wales, is a further factors. Small-scale studies, able to identify some of the processes of classrooms, may produce very specific information related to teachers and such triangulation again demands studies of some scope and scale. Observation of the SATs themselves is a key element in Key Stage 1 researches, and because of the limited window of time within which the SATs are administered, there are physical problems in large-scale sampling for observational research.

Development of standard assessment tasks and tests

The development of standard task and subsequently test materials for respectively Key Stages 1 and 3 has been one sponsored area of research/ development. Such development has worked closely to specifications by SEAC. The early work for Key Stage 1 and the 1990 pilots suggested ambitious schemes, with a high concentration on construct and content validity. The Standard Tests and Assessment Implementation Research consortium used a network of teachers to develop and trial activities for each Statement of Attainment at Key Stage I. All three Key Stage I development consortia were required to conduct a 2 per cent sample pilot nationally using their materials and to publish reports on these across specified areas including relative performance by gender and ethnicity. The ambitiousness of some of the early development work has been progressively reduced through the concerns with 'manageability' and 'the question of what it is most efficient to assess'. Assessing all pupils appears to have been a priority for SEAC in its monitoring of the pilots. This coverage is essential to a programme of national testing to provide school league tables but not necessary to the expressed purposes of training teachers and providing them with a means of checking their standards.

LEAs' role in providing training, support and moderation of Key Stage 1 SATs is complemented also by an evaluative role of its own arrangements. SEAC has gathered information by proforma from LEAs. Moderators (later called 'auditors') are advised to gather information on the training and support given to teachers, on the assessment procedures, teachers' perceptions of the reliability of results, the 'consistency between one school and another' and on whether the National Curriculum assessment is 'proving beneficial to the children's education' and it is unclear whether it refers to consistency of standard of assessment or procedural consistency in carrying out assessments, or even consistency in curricular practice.

HMI reports

HMI in a *Survey of 100 Schools* reported on the implementation of the National Curriculum in primary schools in 1989, and commented upon strategies for observation, methods of record keeping and attention to progression. Records they noted were generally improving in their standardization and curricular coverage, and some schools were recording not only the work that whole classes had covered, but also individual progress. They also, however, noted a proliferation of checklists providing 'only superficial information.

Subsequent reports covering Key Stage 1, 2 and 3, and relating to core subjects individually and to Special Educational Needs, were more searching in relation to progression and continuity. In relation to special needs students in ordinary schools they again criticize the checklist approach: 'Such systems rarely influenced the planning of future work. The Science report draws attention to the fact that recording has been a priority at the expense of 'ways of matching performance to levels in a consistent manner...' and recommends that schools give more attention to 'using the results of assessment to guide the planning of future work'. The Mathematics report emphasizes the need to 'ensure that information obtained is used to plan the next stage in the pupils' developmen. The English report focuses upon poorly differentiated work and the fact that 'Some departments confused the recording of experiences with the assessment of what had been achieved'. This report too is concerned with progression: 'A lack of connection between assessment and subsequent planning was widespread.' The use of written comments for diagnosis was also generally lacking.

Ofsted had taken over this reporting role by the 1993 report on the 1991-92 year. Its report on *Assessment, Recording and Reporting* is based on 2600 inspections across primary and secondary schools. Their claims that Key Stage 1 assessment is now firmly established...' and 'In Key Stage 3, teachers and pupils came successfully through the national pilot tests, despite a good deal of public anxiety...' give no indication of the tensions that led to industrial action and a widespread boycott of SAT and test procedures in 1993, and again in 1994. There is a general message that there were improvements over the previous year, but the basis of these improvements is often on grounds of administration and manageability: 'Many Year 2 teachers were better prepared to administer the Standard Assessment Tasks in 1992 than in 1991. Schools benefited from the previous year's experience'. 'Schools found the 1992 Standard Tasks easier to manage than those used in 1991'. 'The decision not to assess investigative work in Science and Mathematics through the Standard Tasks simplified administration and reduced the overall time needed'. 'Teachers generally made more reliable assessments than in 1991. This was partly because the 1992 Standard Tasks were more manageable'. Where there were matters to criticize, these were apparently problems with teachers not with the Tasks: 'Administering the Tasks to small groups at a time also showed up the wider weaknesses in teachers' ability effectively to manage learning in small groups'

The reporting on Key Stage 3 refers to pilot tests run in Science and Mathematics in 1991. The report does not directly address the issue of how far the Key State 3 tests are intended to mirror the practices of examinations at 16+, though there is some assumption of an examination culture:

> Most schools provided opportunities for pupils to practise for the tests, although the amount of preparation and revision varied significantly from school to school. Some departments prepared revision materials and class work tests that were clearly linked to relevant ATs, sometimes using SEAC's sample materials as a guide. This kind of preparation had a beneficial effect on pupils' subsequent results...A few teachers overdid the pupils' preparation and undertook intensive cramming which caused unnecessary anxiety...

The report does not engage with whether the revision and preparation that stopped short of 'cramming' had beneficial effects on students' motivation for learning or their longer term understanding of the material. There is a section devoted to 'Managing the tests' concerned with arrangements for secure storage and for invigilation, and arrangements for pupils needing additional support.

The difficulties are, in short, seen in a predominantly administrative light, with limited exploration of how the process or content of external testing really interacts with teacher development and teaching process. A few potential problems are acknowledged:

There is a danger that the Tasks may be replicated in lessons and give too narrow a focus to the work... not all teachers recognised the potential of good assessment for raising standards, not used assessment to modify their planning and teaching.

These could be seen as fairly fundamental problems in the system, undermining the supposed diagnostic and developmental purposes of the testing.

Reports on pilots and the 1992 Key Stage 1 assessment commissioned by SEAC

The Evaluation of the National Curriculum at Key Stage 1 (ENCA) project based at the University of Leeds expands the brief to take account of contextual school and classroom factors, 'to provide explanations as to why and discrepancies of scores between TA, SAT and ENCA re-assessment occurred'.

The study sampled 96 schools from 16 LEAs with some balance of metropolitan/non-metropolitan location and geographical location defined by North, South, East and West regions of the country. Within that sample, numbers of children were identified according to age, gender, ethnic background, first language and social background. The study also collected as contextualizing information details of teachers' and headteachers' length of service and qualifications.

The strands of data collection were observational studies, ENCA re-assessments, questionnaires to LEAs, to teachers, pupils and parents, and pupil record sheets. Their report concludes that there was some unevenness of preparation for assessment across the country between LEAs. They found discrepancies between teachers in their understandings of terms in SoAs, most particularly in English where in such terms as 'fluency' and 'understanding' they found 'little agreement'. In Mathematics and Science a more common area of discrepancy was between teachers and SAT developers in their interpretation of 'or' in SoAs. Teachers commonly took this to mean that items were alternatives whereas SATs treated the listings as inclusive of its items.

This study found higher correlation between SAT scores and teacher assessments in schools which had experience of the 1990 pilots, suggesting the importance of experience and familiarity.

Such findings appear to endorse the need for further LEA coordination and training, and that agreement about interpretation of such statements is the result of shared experience over time rather than of written publication or single training events. They also attribute some of the discrepancies between SAT scores and TAs to unfamiliarity of teachers with levels.

The report gives, however, support to the TAs and offers its judgement that some of the discrepancies between sets of scores arose from the greater curriculum coverage of TAs. Furthermore, they cast doubt on the extent to which conditions can be 'standard' for SATs: 'If this is taken to imply that the activities, procedures and performance requirements were the same for all children then the 1991 SAT fell considerably short of this'. They found that while the majority of parents (57 per cent) favoured reporting of TA and SAT results, less than 1 per cent favoured the reporting of the SAT result only; 37 per cent favoured the reporting of the TA assessment and not the SAT, a finding that also relates to the teachers' own confidence in their assessments. This confidence is, however, questioned by the discrepancies found between TAs and SAT results where the SAT result was most frequently one level (and sometimes two levels: this study found somewhat more discrepancy than the NFER study) higher than the TA.

ENCA found that in the opinion of headteachers the SAT exercise had a positive effect on relationships between the schools and their governors and parents, but a negative effect on general behaviour. There was concern by teachers and others about the non-challenging nature of work for those children not involved in SATs. Children's perceptions of the tasks and of their performance suggested some positive views but this information is not cross-referenced with information about actual performance, and therefore is unable to shed light on questions about the extent to which pupils' understanding about assessment may affect the curricular impact of assessments.

The study also found that age of children appeared to be affecting their achievement of levels. There were also gender differences, particularly in English where girls were achieving significantly better than boys, as also in some ATs in Science and

Mathematics. Performance in English and Mathematics they found to be significantly better in pupils who had nursery experience. They found differences in groups according to ethnic origin with the lowest performance among Asian children and the highest among white children (the groupings for this were very broad) and that there was 'a declining pattern of attainment for children from high status neighbourhoods to low status neighbourhoods'.

The ENCA re-assessments do not appear to have contributed greatly to the study with the most important sources of data coming from questionnaires, SAT and TA information. The ENCA re-assessments were not able to sample validly across the curriculum and therefore offer data which can only be considered alongside the other data rather than as a reference point from which to judge it. They were carried out later than the other assessments and by people unknown to the children and the report acknowledges that it is not possible to know whether this would have had positive or negative effects upon performance.

The study carried out by NFER/BGC retained some distinction between the strands of its research into teacher assessment on the one hand and the SATs on the other. The research into teacher assessment was conducted by questionnaire, nationally, and by visits to 38 schools from 24 LEAs. The schools were selected to 'elucidate particular issues'. The consortium's study of SATs also sampled nationally by questionnaire to teachers and by requesting a stratified sample of schools to send pupil record sheets pupil information and assessment record booklets, and had response rates of between 50 and 70 per cent for various materials and parts of the sample.

The study gives attention to workload, collecting information about the additional hours spent by teachers on planning for SATs, administering them and preparation during the SAT period. The overload identified is offered as a possible explanation for some of the incorrect routes taken through the SATs. They also collected information about relative levels of confidence of teachers before and during the SATs and found that levels rose in the course of the exercise. Since they identified high levels of anxiety before the SAT exercise it is difficult to equate the SAT procedures with an increase in confidence when what may have been experienced is relief rather than professional growth.

They found acceptable facility values, but with some discrepancy in performance across SoAs. There was general correlation between ATs the notable exception being handwriting which correlated poorly with other English ATs and with Science and Mathematics performance. They found there were discrepancies in level between TA and SAT results, 'the most frequent discrepancy was for the Standard Assessment task result to be one level higher than the TA'. They found that there was an improvement in match of TA and SAT levels compared with the 1990 pilots, with an average match of 57 per cent in English, 41 per cent in Mathematics, 31 per cent in Science and 63 per cent in Welsh. Familiarity would again seem to be important, but, unlike the ENCA study they found that the match in assessments among the 1990 pilot schools was no greater than among other schools.

The study used resolved results to consider whether there were significant differences among groups. They found a similar pattern to ENCA with girls performing higher across the English ATs than boys and in some ATs in the other core subjects. They too found an age advantage. Asian and Afro-Caribbean children were more frequently achieving at Level 1 than white children. They point out, however, that the sample size in relation to ethnicity is too small to permit reliable inferences. Unlike the ENCA study they found no consistent evidence of advantage from nursery experience. They also present tentatively some findings on small classes in which there appeared to be an 'increased likelihood of achievement at Level 3', but suggest that this would require further investigation using multi-level modeling.

NFER and Brunel University carried out a study of the Key Stage 3 pilot assessments in Mathematics and Science in 1992. Their sampling matrix consisted of school type, size of age group and location (metropolitan/non metropolitan, and by one of four broadly defined regions of the country - North, Midlands, South, Wales). Schools were surveyed by questionnaire, with a pupil sample of 12 per school providing the data for analysis of performance. There were also case-study visits related to particular topics such as reactions to the testing process.

Their study identified a number of points for development, both in relation to the support needed for teacher assessment, and in relation to coverage, validity and reliability of tests. There is attention to administration, to sources of bias, and to teacher and pupil reactions to the tests. It is a detailed report, mainly concerned, in accordance with its brief, with fine-tuning of a system intended to be fully operational for the following year. It does also engage, however, in some more wide-ranging discussion of the 'State of Development of National Curriculum Assessment'. The original TGAT concept of a parallel formal assessment to those made by teachers for all attainment targets has been lost. As currently operating, the formal test element of National Curriculum assessment at Key Stage 3 can now be seen to be the result of a series of decisions to reduce the amount of time needed for assessment and to focus on summative pu:poses. In our view a reappraisal is needed of the purposes. In our view a reappraisal is needed of the purposes of the Key Stage 3 tests so that all are clear on these purposes and the tests are designed to meet them...Highly aggregated data available for all pupils could be acquired by simpler tests designed to produce a subject level. More detailed monitoring of standards could be accomplished by an effective strategy of sampling schools...We recommend that SEAC consider in detail the level and nature of the information required from the Key Stage 3 testing programme and ensure that clearly stated purposes are met by producing an assessment framework designed to produce this information as efficiently and reliably as possible.

Reports on the implementation of Mathematics in the National Curriculum, Science and English were also commissioned, based on national surveys and more detailed case-study research. Though these reports have curriculum as their central focus they also, naturally, identify a number of issues relating to assessment: 'many of the problems relate to the dual nature of the current Mathematics Order in attempting to provide a framework to guide teaching and a prescription for assessment arrangements'. The Science reports include detailed consideration of progression and differentiation, both closely related to good formative assessment practice. 'The prevailing debate and concerns about assessment tend to place the summative functions of assessment to the fore. There has been relatively little discussion about the development and use of diagnostic tests that support the on-going teaching of science'. Moreover, the development of Key Stages (essentially driven by the idea of key reporting stages for summative results) 'has probably resulted in a greater within-phase introspection. There is a paradox here, since one of the National Curriculum innovations was to set out the courses of study that would enhance the possibility of continuity across the Key Stage 2-Key Stage 3 divide'. Such continuity, the report suggests, requires processes to support it, and it advocates the kinds of study groups that had been established for the research as a model for such development. The report on differentiation identifies similarly the need for processes of teacher support to realize the curricular aims of assessment.

Formative assessment provides an essential underpinning to effective differentiation. This is a skill which is part of good classroom practice, but which teachers need support in developing. This should be addressed by in-service training, but further there is a need for more active and participatory forms of teacher development. Effective differentiation cannot proceed simply by prescribing a list of strategies for teachers to adopt...Teacher involvement in empirical classroom-based research should be undertaken in order to explore approaches towards differentiated provision. Such research should help to identify successful teaching strategies that can improve the quality of learning experiences offered to all pupils. The research outcomes would inform professional guidance an INSET provision.

Following the substantial boycott of the Key Stage 3 tests in England and Wales in 1993, as well as a widespread boycott of Key Stage 1 SATs, Ron Dearing was charged by the DFE with the task of reviewing the National Curriculum and its assessment arrangements. The terms of reference of the review were:

(i) the scope for slimming down the curriculum;

(ii) how the central administration of the National Curriculum and testing arrangements could be improved.

(iii) how the testing arrangements might be simplified; and

(iv) the future of the ten-level scale for recognising children's attainment.

The review was conducted through consultations ranging across teacher associations, parents groups and industry, and also through regional conferences for consultation with teachers. Although the Dearing proposals have meet mixed reactions from those in education, the involvement of teachers so actively in the consultations was in itself a significant shift in the policy of implementation and review by government. In a letter from Ron Dearing to the Secretary of State for Education:

> I have been deeply impressed - at times moved - by the strong commitment of everyone concerned in education to serve our children well...the last thing our schools need is precipitate, ill-thought through change.

The slimming down of the curriculum opens the way for much more variety in the post-14 age group and for the introduction of vocational qualification. It also reduces the workload elsewhere. After a circumspect discussion of the 10-level scale, it is decided that it should be retained, as preferable to Key Stage gradings which were proposed as the main alternative. It has been suggested in Chapter 10 that the increased flexibility in the curriculum brought about by the slimming down will in itself by significant in establishing the context for other kinds of curriculum development in the later 1990s. The other area of significance is the whole change in tone about the role of teachers, and the acknowledgement that there may need to be a more active role for teachers in moderating processes for teacher assessment in non-core subjects for which statutory tests are not now to be developed. Although he envisages a role for non-statutory tests and guidance materials, and for inspection visits in the moderating process, he also makes the 'assumption that schools in a locality come together to form groups to moderate their assessments'.

ESRC research and evaluation studies

Two ESRC (Economic and Social Research Council) - funded projects will be briefly outlined here: The

Primary Assessment, Curriculum and Experience Project based at Bristol Polytechnic and Bristol University and National Assessment in Primary Schools Evaluation Project based at the London Institute of Education.

The PACE project was a longitudinal study, giving it greater depth and continuity of contact with study schools than the SEAC-commissioned work. Its sample of 50 schools across eight LEAs is for the purposes of some strands of its methodology reduced to a sub-sample of 10. Its sampling is described as drawing on a range of schools, by geographical location; in terms of strategies of LEA support and coordination and in terms of socio-economic factors. Its methodology comprised: structured interviews with headteachers and infant teachers; classroom observation and discussion of the sub-sample of schools; detailed monitoring of assessment within that sub-sample; an ethnography to identify features of the schools as a whole; and a federated approach to collating the outcomes of action research projects of teachers offering to be attached to the project as a whole.

The findings of the project, as well as its developing practice (for it is also engaged in exploring methodological issues in relation to the study of national assessments) have been published in a series of working papers. One of these is outlined here to indicate key themes that emerged in the research.

Broadfoot and others identify a range of issues which could loosely be categorized as pedagogic, organizational, technical (in relation to making assessments), and concerning relations with colleagues and parents.

The paper focuses upon time pressures, support needed to carry out SATs effectively in the classroom, disruption of normal practice, the tensions caused by a shift from collaborative and teacher-supported work, neglect of non-SAT children and teachers' emphasis on the need to protect children from stress. These issues represent organization matters but are also a great deal deeper, as they interrelate with closely held views about the nature of classroom relations and the way those support effective learning. Views of teachers about the assessments made using SATs showed a concern about the following: the absence of formative/diagnostic information; lack of faith in resolved levels in some cases; lack of standard conditions; wide variety of achievement in some levels-the tasks not differentiating effectively); problems in making decisions about level; and some issues of validity, for example that the time constraint in a Mathematics task did not appear to be relevant to the SoA. Teachers also identified that the SATs presented new features in their relationship with parents, in terms of parental preceptions of SATs' purposes, the need to calm some parents' anxieties about testing, and the problems some parents perceived when other parents were helping in SAT classrooms. Relationships with collegues were feared by some to be affected, since there were anxieties that there might be disagreements over levels.

The study of SATs is, of course, only one element in the much larger developing picture of national assessment addressed by the PACE project, though some of the themes identified are common to the whole of the national Curriculum assessment procedure. Boradfoot and others give prominence to record-keeping and pupils' involvement in the process of recording, and to ownership, themes which are consonant with Records of Achievement and suggest an integrated way forward, and 'evidence that we might be at the beginning of a very creative phase of development in the use of assessment'.

The project questions the reliability of the SATs at Key Stage 1, and finds evidence contrary to the views of Ofsted that experience is necessarily making assessments more valid and reliable:

During the 1992 assessment process too, all Pace schools were visited while the Mathematics 3 SAT, which seems to purport to be more reliable that those used in 1991, was carried out. Observation suggested, however, that this apparently more standardised task was equally vulnerable to variations in the way teachers present the activity.

The London Institute study involved four LEAs, with a stratified random sample of eight schools within each. The research was conducted by discussion, interview and observation (Gipps *et al.* 1992). The issues identified for interim discussion were: school organization; teaching and ancillary support; support by head-teachers; quality of support; stress, especially of Year 2 teachers and headteachers; curricular implications of assessment practices; school development; changes in classroom practice, for example there was greater use of group-work; and the degree of integration of SATs into normal classroom practice. The emergent themes identified from the findings under these headings are teachers' emphasis on protecting children, encouraging best performance feelings of guilt and anxiety and a sense of raised professionalism.

What we can say is that the 1991 KS1 SATs were designed on an authentic assessment model. Despite anxiety over the quality of the worksheets, they matched the active process-based tasks which children do in good infant classroom practice much more closely than do traditional standardized tests. As our data shows, these assessment tasks not only gave our teachers direct ideas for areas of the curriculum which they had not covered, but also, for some, pointers towards a wider view of teaching and learning. This is the opposite of a traditional view of teaching to the test - which is typically viewed as narrowing and negative - in that it widened teachers' practice rather than narrowed it. Thus, from this experience we can say that the introduction of high-stakes, authentic assessment can broaden teachers' practice...On this basis, we can hypothesize that the move away from using process-based tasks and any attempt to return to narrow paper and pencil test of the traditional, standardized type will effect a narrowing of teaching again.

An administrative, technical, pedagogic and political issue?

The reports from HMI and Ofsted, and those reports working to SEAC terms of reference, give considerable attention to administration and manageability of the SAT, testing and teacher assessment arrangements. That focus tends to cast other more fundamental issues aside, and does not address the validity of the exercise which is to be made less time-consuming. There is a danger that some reporting on assessment looks at manageability, at the expense of purpose.

The technical issues surrounding assessment, particularly of the validity and reliability of the assessments, of whether there are any sources of bias in the assessments and how results should be interpreted, are clearly important ones. Apart from the critical attention received in some of the work quoted here, there have also been other studies addressing the principles of assessment and reporting. For example, Cresswell and Houston argue that the problems of decontextualized assessment, and of aggregation of levels, indicate the appropriateness of a profiling of National Curriculum assessments are Key Stage 4.M. Brown discusses the inappropriateness of reporting the subject level as the median of the levels achieved across Attainment Targets as likely to give a very inaccurate picture of achievement. These are clearly very importance matters, central to retaining the vitality of the claim that national assessment arrangements can truly provide valid diagnostic information.

The ESRC-sponsored projects outlined above, together with those reports published by SCAA regarding implementation of the curriculum in specific subjects, have a strong concern with pedagogy, the effects of assessments upon classroom activities and the extent to which assessment arrangements do - or can - inform the processes of teaching and learning.

The key issue that the research on National Curriculum assessment raises, however, is one of level. the context for National Curriculum assessment is not easy to reduce. The political and social change of the late twentieth century give a new prominence to education as a principal site of a complex struggle between professional privilege. commercial pragmatism and community rights. To locate assessment research within particular issues, or (as may increasingly happen in the secondary range) within subject discipline-based areas of study, risks removing it from its centrality in such a struggle. The use of research on Key Stage I pilots (showing them to be unwieldy, time-consuming and subject to unequal amounts of school-based resourcing) to justify governmentally prescribed simplification of the tasks to timed tests is indicative of the political context in which such research currently operates.

McNamara, outlining an 'agenda for research', draws attention to the political context: educational researchers are only noticed 'where it is convenient for those who determine events to quote "research" to justify policies which they are determined to pursue in any event'. He suggests that in such a context the way forward for educational research is rather to engage with the Government's claim that the Education Reform Act will improve the quality of learning in schools but lays down a National Curriculum which is eloquently silent on how such an aspiration is to be attained.

Gipps argues that there is a lack of fundamental research particularly accompanying the introduction of assessment: 'Millions of pounds have so far been spent on national assessment and yet the programme itself is in a shambles' (Gipps 1991a: 277). She outlines the areas, spanning fundamental research and development and monitoring, which should, she argues, be the focus of the research effort: process-based criterion-referenced assessment, performance assessment, organization and pedagogical issues, learning hierarchies, the use of assessment results and equal opportunities (1992a: 277-86). Brown makes a similar defence of the importance of fundamental research 'within the framework of the current, somewhat frenetic, activity' (S. Brown 1991:238).

Fundamental research is, however, seriously challenged by current policy, and not only by funding allocation, but also because of the way in which research findings are seen through the lens of policy. There are also features of current change which are consciously designed to challenge the strongholds of Higher Education, and to expose the weaknesses of the fragmentation that specialization can cause within institutions, and indeed nationally in research. The question remains of whether the National Curriculum assessment can or should be considered out of the context of radical change in schools brought about by Local Management of Schools, and whether teaching and learning are indeed separable from the entire social context in which education is currently a central and embattled part.

15 Total Quality Management in Education and Training Context

Defining quality

Philip Crosby, an American quality "guru", defines quality as, "Everyone in the Company from the doorman to the managing director, routinely doing things right".

This is a helpful, but in one respect a puzzling, definition of quality for Further Education and Training. It is in taking what is helpful, and in grappling with what is puzzling, that further education establishments can find a direction to move forward on a coherent and planned approach to assuring and improving quality.

I imagine that no-one in education would quarrel with the assertion that everyone within the organization should be involved in the drive for quality. Students attend or interact with colleges in a variety of ways and have a complex range of expectations and needs which they require the college to fulfil; these may range from the achievement of defined learning outcomes, to personal development, social satisfaction, counselling and guidance and will undoubtedly include the expectation of courteous and efficient service in all of their dealings with the college. Clearly, everyone employed by the college will affect the quality of the student's experience.

Neither is there initially any difficulty with the notion of "routinely doing things right". At the first level of understanding this expresses a commitment to delivering each part of our service on a fight first and every time basis. Anything less would imply an acceptance of sloppy work and inferior standards.

However the problem arises when we examine the notion of the meaning of right in education and training. Our core technology, the enabling of learning, is a complex and interactive process and a simple exhortation to get things right begs the fundamental question - What is right in education and training?

There are numerous and frequently changing interpretations of what constitutes a quality learning experience; these may be subject to political dogma, changing fashions in education technology and pressures from stake holders other than the learner. A tempting solution to this dilemma would be to limit or quality assurance to those elements of our service which would be easier to describe and quantify; it is right and laudable that such aspects of our service are included in any quality improvement process but to ignore the fundamental issue of the quality of learning would be to relegate quality to the periphery of our activities and would fail to capture the imagination of our teaching staff.

Given that learning is an interactive process and that, in the literature of Total Quality Management, quality is seen as meeting the requirements and expectations of the customer, a way forward becomes clear - we consult those who intimately involved, the learners. By a process of negotiation between the suppliers (the staff of the college) and the customers (the students) we can arrive at an explicit and realistic set of quality requirements that we can guarantee to achieve.

But unlike other service industries, the qualify of our "product", the learning outcome, is not wholly within our control. We can only control our processes. The learner's contribution is vital and therefore should form part of the stated quality requirements. Thus, by negotiation we will arrive at a quality contract or a quality entitlement owned by the learner and the college. This contract will guarantee certain services, processes and behaviors so that the student an the college staff will fully understand what to expect from each other. The aspiration would be negotiated quality requirements with each learner but at first it may only be possible to arrive at negotiated quality requirement for groups of students.

Thus the quality we assure is realistic within resources, meets our customer's reasonable expectations, is owned by the customer and the supplier and is achievable. By stating specific requirements we can measure achievement and plan to improve on any shortcomings.

Quality is performing to requirements each and every time.

Planning to achieve quality

Total Quality Management is concerned with people, system and culture.

It is a truism that people are any organisation's most valuable resource but, in the context of quality improvement and assurance in education and training, it is worth repeating. Management's task within TQM is to create a situation in which the commitment, flair and experience of the staff can be released and guided to meet the agreed requirements of the customer. It is essential that senior managers themselves are trained in the philosophy and practices of TQM prior to committing to a programme of quality improvement. the genuine involvement of all in negotiating quality requirements, planning to achieve those requirements, identifying problems and offering and implementing solutions will be exiting but challenging and it's all too easy to retreat into hierarchical and authoritarian behaviour when the rhetoric becomes the reality of genuine involvement and problem identification. Management commitment must be visible, genuine and ongoing.

Management commitment is demonstrated by;

- generating the quality policy through consultation
- publicising the quality policy
- allocating money and time to the quality process
- attending quality team meetings
- taking with staff both informally and formally about quality
- modelling the quality culture
- valuing and respecting people all of them, all of the time)

- insiting on clear quality requirements and documented procedures

At the beginning of the quality improvement process, managers will need to win their staff's commitment to, involvement with and awareness of quality by providing an opportunity for them to agree and make explicit the shared values of the organisation. Secondly, they will need to set up systems for team working and open. communication. the notion that quality is achieved by the requirements of the customer is equally applicable to customer/supplier relationships within an institution as it is to the external customer and supplier. Therefore teams will be most effective if based on these internal customer supplier relationships. The teams will be able to work together to agree quality requirements for specific services or functions, plan the work processes to ensure that these requirements are met, identify where errors or problems are occurring, devise and suggest solutions to these problems and act to eliminate the error. They will need to feel secure that this work will be regarded as positive and commendable and to know that there a reformat and safe channels of communication by which problems and solutions can be communicated the line and whole college managers and decision making bodies. Having established these quality improvement teams and channels of communication managers will need to ensure that the team members have been trained in the skills and techniques of work process analysis, problem identification and solving and collaborative group working. It will also be advantageous to establish a team of staff who have an overarching leadership, advice and support function in the quality improvement process. The members of this team will need to be representative of all of the working groups and management levels within the college and will need in depth training in quality philosophy, systems and techniques. IN support of these activities there will be a need to provide systems to document defined quality requirements and working procedures.

Expert advice and training on assurance and monitoring system should be sought. Wherever possible these functions should be in the control of the quality improvement and audit process must involve customer consultation on their level of satisfaction on the achievement of quality requirements. The quality loop will then ensure that corrective action is taken where a failure to meet a requirement has been identified.

An essential prerequisite for success in the quality improvement programme is the creation of an organisational culture that is supportive of the aims and process of total quality. The first step for this will have been taken by involving all staff in the identification and expression of shared organisational values. There are some cultural characteristics which are essential to enable the process to succeed. Perhaps most vital of these is a real commitment to a no blame culture. Open communication is also a vital ingredient with everyone believing that a genuine attempt will be made to understand and to trust the intentions of the communicators. The culture will also be one in which its is expected that people will act; education is all too prone to analysing problems and spending an inordinate amount of time and energy on finding the intellectually and ideologically pure solution only to move on to the next problem before corrective action has been taken. Thus at all levels there will need to be a commitment to act, or at the very least to respond even if only to explain why a suggested solution cannot be implemented, within a specified and short time scale.

Thus a total quality culture will have: shared values, commitment to always getting right, open and explicit communication, time for teamwork, training in quality, total involvement, sensitivity to others' needs.

One college's experience of implementing total quality

Background Information

Mid Cornwall and Saltash Colleges had, supported by a county wide project, developed systems and expertise in some aspects of quality assurance through a process of customer consultation based on student questionnaires adapted by course teams from work undertaken in Avon. The students were consulted, in detail, on their satisfaction with access arrangements (everything up to settling into the course), on the quality of their learning and assessment experiences and the validity of their course for the next stage of their lives (further or higher education or employment). Employers and/or further and higher education would also be consulted at the validity stage. The information gained as an aid to action planning for improvement.

A number of full time courses had implemented this approach and the desire was to spread the process to all full and part time courses.

The college management team had consciously decided not to seek course evaluation feedback from the customer consultation processes as they wished, at least in the pilot phase, to ensure that course teams owned the process and the information and that staff did not feel threatened or defensive.

However, after the first year of the project, the course teams themselves felt that they would like to have clear ways of communicating information and requests to management at least about those issues which could be resolved by management or whole institution decision making groups.

There was also a feeling by key members of the management team that the time was right to implement a whole college quality system both in response to an internal desire to d so and in response to external pressures. The College wished to develop and implement a quality approach which matched its culture rather than adopt a prescribed quality management system such as ISO 9000. They were attracted by what they had learned of TQM and by the notion of continuous, or incremental quality improvement

Some funding was available from a Regional Department of Employment project.

Beginning the Process

The College's management team decided to use a consultant to assist them with the initial stages of investigating TQM, to provide some management training in TQM and to help facilitate the introduction of their chosen approach to the whole staff of the College.

The first activity was a development day for the College management team in which they explored the essential concepts of TQM and used TQM techniques to generate a draft College Quality Policy and draft College Quality Aims.

The second phase was to consult the College Governors who had a crucial role in management commitment and an evening session for managers and governors was held in which a presentation on quality systems in general and in education was made. The focus was on TQM as providing a framework which fitted College culture, which could if required embrace ISO 9000 and which could build on the work undertaken by the course teams in integrating regular and rigorous customer consultation into course review process. During structured discussion, following the presentation, governors supported the approach that was recommended. Additionally a high degree of experience in industrial applications of TQM was identified and their assistance was enlisted with the next phase of programme.

The third phase was to launch the TQM programme with the whole College staff. An afternoon ad evening session was organised to which all full time staff and part time employees who worked more than ten hours per week were invited. Management commitment to the programme was effectively demonstrated by the large investment of resources that such an event entailed, by the closing of the College for the afternoon and by the high profile that they took during the proceedings.

Presentations by two College Governors with industrial experience of TQM, by the consultant and by the College Principal and vice Principal (Development) were made and questions sought. Workshop sessions followed in which staff were asked to comment on the draft Quality Policy and the draft Quality Aims and to identify key areas within the College that should be the subject of the first phase of the quality improvement programme.

Following this session with all staff the suggestions for areas for quality improvement were circulated and staff were invited to volunteer to be involved in the work. The College Quality Policy and Aims were approved by the Board of Governors and circulated to all staff.

A structure for teams was agreed and established with the overarching role being taken by a Quality Steering Group and with for Quality Improvement Groups to address the four areas for whole College improvement that had been identified. It was decided that a regular Quality Newsletter would be produced and distributed to staff.

The College also devised and administered a Quality Audit in the form of an attitude survey with all staff. It is intended to sue the results of the survey to inform management but also as a benchmark against which the results of the whole College Quality Improvements Groups' work can be measured.

Training in some of the tools and techniques of TQM and in group working was undertaken by the College management team. They have begun to cascade this training to members of the Quality Improvement Groups.

16 Educational Standards and Effectiveness

Standards

The difficulty in talking about standards is that the concept is, like 'truth', or 'goodness', or 'beauty', both logically indispensable and yet impossible to define without considerable philosophical elaboration.

The term 'standards' has gathered around itself a web of meanings. Gipps suggests that the term 'standards' is probably more loosely use than any other in education', and she identified its use in three separate ways, which as she points out, range from the very particular notion of the performance of an individual in a specific context to very large social and moral issues. She sees the three uses as attainment - either in basic skills or more widely across the curriculum, levels of educational provision and matters of conduct and social behaviour:

Referring to levels of *attainment* in basic skills such as reading or maths, or levels of attainment in a much wider range of school activities; we may be talking about standards of *provision*, e.g. the number of teachers and books per child, or we may be talking about behaviour, dress and other *social phenomena*.

In the absence of a clear or shared public view of what constitutes 'standards', the term may all too easily come to be equated with examinations and 'result', *Better Schools*, for example, allied the raising of standards closely to school examinations, As well as raising 'standards across the whole ability range', examinations should:

support improvements in the curriculum and in the way in which it is taught;

provide clear aims for teachers and pupils, to the benefit of both and of higher education and employers;

record proven achievement;

promote the measurement of achievement based on what candidates know, understand and can do;

broaden the studies of pupils in the 4th and 5th secondary years and of 6th form students.

These claims are offering a justification for a prescribed curriculum and for the use of what might be termed 'graded objectives'. The shape of the curriculum in its two dimensions is here established: the subjects and the way in which progress in each subject is to be defined. The kind of access outlined could be envisaged as an improvement in standards in its own right, an improvement in provisional and entitlement. Here, however, access is linked only to attainment, and presumably to the idea that readily monitorable average will rise.

Such a narrow view of access raises questions about whether uniformity of provision is truly opportunity, and whether the prescriptiveness of the

National Curriculum is any more than a means of establishing bureaucratic accountability. The final point might serve to confirm this, as the term 'checking' hardly suggests any subtlety of pedagogic model. If, as the paragraphs goes on to suggest, assessment truly yields formative information, then individual progress might reasonably be expected to improve; but if assessment is only perceived to be an exercise in accountability then there are no precedents for supposing that standards in any meaningful sense of the word can be raised.

The idea that rests can measure standards in education is one thing. The idea that testing can raise standards is quite another, yet this has received even less critical attention.

Hartnett and Naish saw the main thrust of the National Curriculum arrangements as 'the claim to provide solutions to complex educational and social problem without additional resources'. They questioned the contention that testing can raise standards, and saw the particular model of standards being used as belonging to 'bureaucratic mode of evaluation' which may be at odds with 'the learning patterns of individual children'.

HMI's inspections of schools have been summarized in annual reports from the Chief Inspector on *Standards in Education*. These reports have focused on certain aspects of what might be termed 'input' - that is on accommodation and equipment, teacher training and supply, on processes (e.g. the teaching of reading), on outcomes (examination results) and on participation rates in post-compulsory education. although the view of standards implicit in the reports ranges quite widely across input, process and results, there are quite narrow definitions of which results are important to highlight.

The isolation by HMI not only of examination results, but of results which did not reflect the ability or advantage of schools' intakes would suggest a very simplistic approach to standards, based on the most accessible data. By HMI were looking at how education authorities used examination results where a number of comparative techniques are mentioned as 'rare', 'isolated instances'. They mention, with some circumspection, the possible value of examination results in monitoring performance and planning of INSET. The report is, however, non-committal about how examination results should - or should not - be interpreted. In view of the National Curriculum 'there is much for LEAs to do in order to put themselves in a position...to make the best use f public examination results...'

The White Paper, a restatement of established strands of the Government's policy. It a restatement of established strands of the Government's policy. It maintained the view that publication of results will somehow drive standards up, but combines this policy with the introduction of inspections. It viewed 'school autonomy and parental choice - combined with the National Curriculum' as the 'keys to achieving higher standards in all schools. There would be increased school accountability through publication of results, providing information about schools' relative performance to inform parental choice. There was to be a new 'School Curriculum and Assessment Authority' - a 'force for raising expectations and standards'. These teams of inspectors, to include lay inspectors from outside teaching and education professions, are aimed to provide 'regular and rigorous inspection under the watchful eye of the new and powerful Chief Inspector for Schools'. Their terms of reference and arrangement for the conduct of inspections is detailed in a *Handbook for the Inspection of Schools,* a document which is available also to schools and for the Inspection of Schools' set out in detail a wide range of indicators and criteria on which evidence is to be collected and judgements made, and hence addresses some of the past criticisms of HMI's treatment of standards in the past, on the grounds of their 'reluctance to explain their research procedures and methodologies'.

The Education (Schools) Act 1992, and the 'Framework' for inspection have established a very public set of criteria about effectiveness. These criteria may not satisfy all commentators on education, and may not successfully probe the ultimate questions about what education is for. They do, however, arguably broaden our the issue of 'standards' from a definition led by results. Moreover, they place the debate about educational effectiveness - and the basis for Ofsted judgements about schools - more firmly in the public arena than was the case with IIMI practices of the past. Questions remain, however, about what effectiveness is, and about the meanings that are set up by particular definitions and by processes of inspection.

School effectiveness

The discussion about schools' effectiveness dates back well before the Government's introduction of legislation designed to impose certain models of effectiveness upon compulsory education. The influential, and controversial study, *fifteen Thousand Hours*, arose from a concern about whether the time pupils spend in school (the fifteen 15000 hours of the title) actually makes a difference to their achievement and attitudes. The study was located in 12 Inner London Education Authority (ILEA) secondary schools. Its method was to relate individual school inputs processes and outcomes, statistically. Its purpose was to look at whether particular aspects of school process actually made a difference to outcomes. It attempted to take into account differing intake factors in its analysis. It claimed to show that it had identified differences attributable to school processes. Its methods, however, attempted to apply statistical analysis to complex classroom processes and its modelling was open to criticism. Subsequent studies have tended to take more qualitative approaches, such as that carried out in 50 ILEA primary schools, set out to identify the characteristics, or 'key factors' of 'effective schools'.

Reid *et al.* drew together research from a number of studies to suggest characteristics of the effective school, but emphasize that the characteristics of effective schools (such as leadership, pupil participation, strength of teaching staff) are not simple hand-ons. They are guidelines which support certain essential commitments of the school to 'the improvement of teaching and learning', to the 'development of the school as a "learning institution"' and to 'the humanisation of schooling'.

The School Management Task Force, with a

remit from the DES, identified a list of factors closely related to what might be seen as the emerging consensus of research and HMI reports: good leadership (i.e. vision and motivation of others); delegation and involvement of staff in policymaking; purposeful staffing structures; well-qualified staff (experience and expertise); clear aims and objectives; effective communication; clear systems of record keeping and assessment; high expectations; coherent curriculum including pupils' experience as a whole; positive ethos; orderly yet relaxed, suitable working environment; evidence of skills in deploying and managing material resources; good relationships with parents and the community; capacity to manage change, solve problems and to develop organically. More important than the characteristics themselves, however, are the statements of purpose: 'The focus of a good school is effective learning: this is the reason for its existence and therefore the final criterion against which its management is judged'. Moreover, their report was centrally concerned with looking at processes for bringing about management development in schools, and saw roles for LEAs, for Higher Education, industry in schools, and saw roles for LEAs, for Higher Education, industry and professional associations; its language is that of 'support', 'collaborate'. 'consultancy and training opportunities' and it envisaged a network of regional Management Task Forces coordinating this development. It is a very different vision from that of external inspections; it establishes a framework for school-based but collaborative development, rather than a framework of judgements and sanctions.

There was also a flurry of work around performance indicators following the introduction of Local Management of Schools. Such 'indicators' are variously defined. They are part of the framework of audit; they may be divided into input, process and outcome indicators; they may need to be consciously electric of different models; they may be 'selected items of quantitative data which help in the evaluation of aspects of quality' in an inspection system. There is a level of agreement among studies that indicators form a profile. This is a level of agreement among studies that indicators form a profile. This profile consists of 'major issue areas of significant and enduring educational importance' - an 'outline; of 'the most important contexts within which those concerned with the management and appraisal of schools might need to identify key factors which contribute to the quality of their performance'.

Both CIPFA (the Chartered Institute of Public Finance and Accountancy) and Coopers and Lybrand in their reports of the late 1980s stress the importance of developing indicators within the working context. The indicators 'will, properly, vary with the perceptions of those in the particular school or LEA ... These papers do not prescribe a list of indicators but identify areas for schools and/or LEA to use in developing *their own* [their emphasis performance indicators'. Coopers and Lybrand suggest that LEA s will play a key role: 'LEAs will...wish to specify minimum requirements for information on financial performance, resources and examination results and other performance indicators'. Their report stands aloof from suggesting a list of indicators, and offers rather a 'List of factors *relevant* to performance indicators'.

Another, distinct, tradition of work on school effectiveness is concerned with looking at the processes for school and teacher development, through action research models of teacher involvement in school improvement. While action research involves targets and criteria (though the language may very) they are derived at an institutional level, through professional discussion. This development tradition derives from the academic study and practice of evaluation, linked closely to the curriculum evaluations of the Schools Council and the increasing move from outsider/ objectivity-reliability focused evaluations to insider evaluations acknowledging multiple subjectivities. It addresses the need for illuminative research capable of representing a learning milieu a 'nexus of cultural, social, institutional and psychological variables'. It advocates action research by practitioners; extending a research approach within schools by teachers into recent educational change as 'a source of critical self-reflection and emancipatory action'; and involving students in discussion about change. In the developmental tradition, involvement and participation become centrally important. The identification of success criteria and various levels of educational objective in evaluation becomes an important process in itself. This is also supported by other, more quantitative research:

It appeared that an efficient system within which teachers worked harmoniously towards agreed goals was conducive to both good morale and effective teaching.

By contrast to 'effectiveness' studies geared either to description or to measurement, the tradition which embraces evaluation, development and action research offers a participative level. Its central concern that educational development has ultimately to be understood at the level of the school, the classroom, the individual, is compatible with the view of Reid *et al.* about the importance of developing the 'learning institution' in which all are involved in process of growth and an ethos of enquiry and development. Similarly, the School Management Task Force identified the need for the school to develop organically. The Education Act 1988 and the Education Act 1992, however, so fundamentally change the context of accountability that a developmental approach is directly threatened by the assessment arrangements that are driving the machine, and by the influence that these arrangements will have upon school's conceptions of purpose and values, or of what, pragmatically, are their priorities.

The publication of examination results and of National Curriculum assessment results has major implications for the way schools see their work, and how they understand their own capacities for judgement and action. Discussion of 'effectiveness', when engaging with the issue of results is in danger of becoming embroiled in discussion of the need for 'contextualization' rather than engaging with the whole issue of the effects of publication on school processes. The arguments for contextualization of these results take two main forms. Firstly, there is the argument that socio-economic factors should be considered: 'Great care is needed with ...

comparisons of performance as the differences between schools and between their socio-economic environments are such that superficiality can be misleading if not dangerous'. Secondly, it is suggested that more useful information about school performance is based on the progress that students make. the 'value-added' model and objections to it have been outlined in Chapter9.

A further issue to address is how far there is a genuine articulation between the discourse of management and a discourse about learning. How are the claims of the School Management Task Force that effective learning is the central focus of an effective school to be realized? Is there an organic relationship between 'management' and 'learning'? Mortimore and Stone outline two views of education which are currently in contention in the discussion of quality: one of education as 'an essentially ethical activity', and the other as an instrumental activity designed to bring about the achievement of specifiable and uncontroversial educational goals, such that the key educational issues are technical and administrative. Reynolds identifies some of the complexity in trying to make judgements about the effectiveness of teaching. He discussed the effect of 'teacher personality' and different educational philosophies, and 'whether different methods may be equally effective when used by different persons'.

How far, then, are effectiveness studies well placed to promote more than a 'technical and administrative' view of the educational task; how far are they engaged with the ethical/political/ pedagogical questions of the classroom, and with the complex array of variables which may create the experienced curriculum of students? Shipman's *The Management of Learning* seeks to combine the discourse of management and the discourse of learning. This is an important enterprise, but the book overlooks very influential constructivist and interactionist theories of learning, and chooses rather to support its case by examples from psychologists who more readily fit the technical view of management. His central concern appears to establish a particular kind of management approach free of 'reactionary' or 'romantic' views of children. Bloom is valued for demonstrating that 'kearning can be managed'. This does not address the concern that some educational practices are being preferred because they are overtly managerial and not because they represent best educational practice.

The fact that discourses about effective learning are separate from discourses about school management and school effectiveness has implications. It raised the possibility that within the micro-politics of schools, teaching, learning and curriculum content may be increasingly marginalized as legitimate centres of interest, while management attention focuses upon the outward expressions of the ethos of the school as a whole. There is not automatic relationship between the 'ethos' of a school and the details of interpersonal relationship which may actually create for students an understanding of the 'event structures' of which they are part as learners.

Another element in this already complex problem of the appropriate mode of study for the work of school, is the introduction of inspection. whereas the work cited earlier on the characteristics of effective schools, or performance indicators for looking at schools was conducted in a context in which these might act as general guides to schools in their development, the external inspections established by the 1992 Act provide a very different context.

The 'Framework' for the Inspection of Schools reflects some of differing constituencies which have voices about education. The Government's concern about efficiency is most sharply focused in the part of the 'Framework' which looks at financial management - the 'efficiency of the school'; that is,

the quality of the financial management and decision-making; the efficiency and effectiveness with which resources are deployed to attain the school's aims and objectives and to match its priorities; the efficiency of financial control': 'the assessment of any steps that are taken by the school to evaluate its cost effectiveness.

The opening sections of the Education Act 1988 and the long-standing concerns of HMI for wide personal development of pupils are reflected in that part of the 'Framework' which sets out criteria for judging the school's effectiveness in promoting 'Pupils' spiritual, moral, social and cultural development's: for example,

Spiritual development relates to that aspect of inner life through which pupils acquire insights into their personal existence which are of enduring worth. It is characterised by reflection, the attribution of meaning to experience, valuing a non-material dimension to life and intimations of an enduring reality.

The 'Framework' does incorporate a very considerable amount of inspection of 'process' (indeed the definition above of spiritual development is unlikely to be accessible to any cross-sectional inspection), and therefore may offer a counterbalance to a results-dominated assessment of schools' performance.

It does, however, require an 'analysis' of results, but the associated technical paper is very unspecific on some key points of analysis.

Schools should be asked to provide any quantified data on the intake's ability or attainment. Standardised test results, for those pupils whose examination results are being analysed, may give inspectors *some insight* [italics added] into the value added by the school as shown in its overall GCSE results.

Given the difficulty that expert statisticians are finding in drawing up suitable models for value-added analysis, 'some insight' may even be an overstatement In the absence of its own method for interpreting results, the paper says: 'Schools should be asked to provide details of any of their own initiatives to analyze value-added factors in their results, and any other evaluations of their own results'. Similarly,

The LEA in whose area the school lies may undertake its own analyses of examination results for that area. Such analyses may be, at present, the only source of information on value-added. Registered Inspectors may wish to seek access to any such analyses...

There is a suggestion here that 'value-added' is relatively unproblematic, and a possible danger that results will be interpreted to mean more - or less - than they do.

However, it also gives considerable emphasis to other aspects of assessment, particularly to the kinds of formative information about pupils' progress which will affect lesson and curriculum planning, and which will affect appropriate access to the curriculum. 'Quality of Learning' is to include.

progress made ... learning skills, including observation and information-seeking, looking for patterns and deeper understandings and ideas in various ways, posing questions and solving problems, applying what has been learned to unfamiliar situation, evaluating work done ... attitudes to learning, including motivation,interest and the ability to concentrate, co-operate the work productivity.

The inspection of 'Assessment, Recording and Reporting' includes the criteria that 'the outcomes are constructive and helpful to pupils, teachers, parents and employers ... the outcomes inform subsequent work' and among the evidence looked for are 'procedures for reviewing and monitoring the progress of individual pupils', and that 'all pupils, irrespective of gender, ability (including giftedness), ethnicity, and social circumstance, have access to the curriculum and make the greatest progress possible. The 'Framwork' thus underlines the importance of good information about achievement and capacities as appropriate access to curriculum and best possible progression for individuals are predicated upon good formative assessment evaluation.

The principles enshrined in the 'Framework' are not at variance with a growing consensus in effectiveness studies about the characteristics which typify 'good schools'. Moreover, it retains a high status for process characteristics of schools (and hence for such otherwise fragile values as formative assessment) in a climate where league tables based on summative assessments are still intended to be the driving force behind school improvement.

The 'Framework' also fulfils the Government's project of 'demystification', and not least for teachers in demystification of criteria on which schools are judged by inspectors. In making explicit, however, it also attempts to separate out various aspects of schools' work and ethos: it presents a different view from the more holistic 'professional' one. Nixon and Rudduck draw attention to the need for criteria and also the possible problems, in an account of research into the transformed role of Local Authority advisors/inspectors:

> advisors/inspectors emphasise the strong element of progressive focusing implicit in the process of school inspection. They tend to shift from ascertaining, what 'bits' of desirable practice are in place to exploring the quality of those 'bits' and the extent to which they add up to something coherent and worthwhile. Concerns about teaching and learning in the classroom might ... occasion a lateral shift of focus to different aspects of school practice - shifts that presuppose a strong sense by advisers/ inspectors of the complex and indeterminate relation between different aspects of school practice.

17 Towards Quality Management in Training Design

Attacking the problems

A member of staff was appointed, and given the necessary independence and authority, to tackle the quality problem. Technical problems that could only have been introduced at the programming stage were the most urgent and important, so a technical production guide was developed to ensure that all concerned were aware of relevant screen design conventions and equipment limitations, and to facilitate communication between designers and programmers. Both internal staff and external subcontractors received copies.

In the meantime observations of defects were being systematically recorded, classified and graded according to criticality, later using Pareto analysis. This allowed informed decisions to be taken about which areas it was possible to standardise. Concurrently, independent reviews were introduced on completion of critical intermediate stages in courseware development, such as the outline design and the programming script. These were intended to trap potential difficulties early enough to prevent their becoming expensive problems.

Thus the classic quality management techniques of process observation, event recording and design review were introduced.

Developing the solution

As a means of specifying technical limitations the technical production guide was a success, but in non-technical matters it didnot reflect a consensus of design views and so was not widely accepted. A parallel investigation of the difficulties of communicating design information showed that in a fast-changing field like training technology, individual projects might have to adopt their own conventions. It became clear that a standards-based approach to quality was valid but would succeed only if environmental influences were taken into account.

Time and cost, of development, observance and enforcement, compared with benefit, help to determine whether or not a standard is issued. So does demand, whether from designers, quality assurance or production staff. What any one standard covers is determined by delivery medium, demand and enforceability, while the principal factors affecting effectiveness are usability and acceptability.

As described above, the first effective standard, the technical production guide, was developed empirically. A pre-release review of a number of CBT courses revealed defects. Classification enabled attention to be given to critical areas and an ideal situation to be determined. Hence a standard for the critical areas could be defined and guidelines issued. The next step was assessment of subsequent projects against the standard.

Currently, when a new standard is required, an example of the item concerned undergoes an initial assessment, by means of inspection, to determine what constitutes a defect. All observations are recorded. The resulting Pareto analysis leads first to revealing what needs standardising, and then to discussions with interested parties and the definition of a standard. Guidelines for new designers are then produced, to help them understand how the standard is intended to be interpreted and in what circumstances exceptions may be advisable. This cycle is repeated as many times as necessary.

The actions described - inspection, recording, analysis, addressing standards, producing guidelines, and assessment, re-inspection or validation - resemble the traditional courseware development cycle and also the classic quality control loop, with the assessor or tester being the sensor and the reference being the standard.

The review at each stage of course development is a logical part of the training validation plan which is built in to each project. It often uses familiar techniques like course piloting with designers' peers or with the target population. Assessment against a standard maybe eased by using checklists and, sometimes, testing plans. It is nevertheless a task requiring a variety of well-developed skills and judgment in the assessor, depending on the medium used for the training. In most areas of training design there will be borderline cases, where technical infringements do not affect training outcomes or would cost a great deal to correct. However, each assessment should produce a record of findings, a correction agenda and a possible improvement action programme.

The road to success

A combination of independent review and acceptably defined standards and well-presented guidelines thus form the foundation of a workable quality management system. Its success requires acceptability, independent assessment and a means of completing the improvement action loop.

Acceptability is assisted by involving project teams closely in the review process and in the definition of standards, and by ensuring that the reviewers are appropriately skilled. The standards themselves must be easy to understand and apply.

Independence is provided through the existence of a quality assurance team whose members, although Lloyds Bank TDG staff, are not members of project teams.

The improvement action loop is addressed by feedback meetings open to all design and production staff. These address specific topics and plan subsequent action, such as a project for writing guidelines.

Quality in alkl training media

In 1991 Training Development Group extended its quality effort to media other than CBT. The techniques described above are now applied to all training design. Guidelines for writers and editors have been produced, and in early 1992 observation data was being gathered from classroom sessions in order to analyse the delivery of face-to-face training.

In the process of extending the system to other media QA staff acquired new skills, and began to be consultants to the four design teams, rather than inspectors. They need skills in writing, editing, proof reading, software testing and interface design, and observation, as well as in quality management. Coaching and giving feedback is important in the review process and good inter-personal skills are vital, as is a full knowledge of the training design and delivery process.

Benefits

Directly quantifiable benefits are discussed in the case study. Among the indirect benefits, the approach is extensible as required, uses many existing skills, can be incorporated into initial project costings and so can be closely monitored, is widely applicable and is sensitive to designers' feelings, External suppliers can easily be involved, without conflicting with their own quality systems. Quality audits can be incorporated, and vast amounts of paperwork are not generated. The visibility of the system is an encouragement to TDG's suppliers and customers alike.

Unlike the approach adopted in BS5750 TDG's approach is not wholly inspection-based and can be implemented fairly gradually in particular areas. Unlike the British Standard also, it is results-based rather than purely activity-based as its primary focus is on improvement action, not fidelity to procedures alone.

Identification

The identification stage can be the part most organisations find difficult to accept. The fact that the identification process is considered necessary indicates there are problems which need addressing, and there is thus room for improvement. As a corollary, this suggests that both processes and people will need to change which can be cause for significant resistance.

Accepting the sensitive position the quality assurance team are in, it is realised that it is not always "what you say" but "how you say it" that counts, and much effort is expended in this type of approach. For instance specific training on coaching and feedback techniques considerably assist this role. In TDG, designers and programmers want to produce better training material and are therefore willing to consider and implement improvement ideas. It is for these reasons QA can feel at ease in offering genuine remedies to common problems and remain confident in the fact they will be welcomed and implemented.

Many inconsistencies (observations) occur throughout CBT production, and the basic method of recording these is on a QA report form. The columns show the observation number (sequential), where in the course the observation occurred, what it was, and recommendations (if any). The "importance" column is described in detail later. The recommendations (if any). The "importance" column is described in detail later. The remaining four columns show the process of correction until final recheck by QA. The forms are not for the sole use of QA members as the designer or other interested parties are actively encouraged to use them.

Each course will generate a number of these forms and therefore a significant number of observations. Following a "brainstorming" session the lengthy "classification of observation" list shown below was produced.

A Key functionality (D)

B Key Functionality (P)

C Help (D)

D Help (P)

E Interactions ie questions (D)

F Interactions ie questions (P)

G Graphics (D)

H Graphics (P)

I Application Simulation (D)

J Application Simulation (P)

K Spelling and Punctuation

L Technical Accuracy

M Tutorial Text (D)

N Tutorial Text (P)

O Mouse

P Observation Readvised

These classifications are intended to cater for all possible inconsistencies likely to be encountered during production of a CBT course and, for clarity, have been assigned individual letters. The (D) and (P) refer to designer and programmer respectively.

Analysis

The analysis stage uses numerous quality management techniques to ascertain the extent (ie frequency) of the observations being made throughout course production, and identify major areas of concern.

A simple "tally chart" was devised to collate and classify the observations from three CBT courses, one internally designed and internally programmed, one externally designed and internally programmed, and one internally designed and externally programmed. This revealed remarkable consistency in the distribution of different types of deficiency.

From the sample of observations from course one, the classification "M" ie Tutorial Text-Design provided the most frequent comments. This is where the programmer has correctly followed the designer's script but for example, a sentence or paragraph does not read correctly, and the observation is consequently highlighted and attributed to the text design. The next highest was the "K" classification with "B" and "F" classifications also featuring highly. The latter two classifications refer to the usability of the keys for navigation throughout the course, and although the design script can sometimes provide incorrect instructions for the programmer, it is more often found that the observation relates to the programming related deficiency.

The second course included a "simulation" of the application as a method of testing the learning. This shows similar priority to course one in terms of Tutorial Text - Design but Key Functionality - Programming came second pushing Spelling and Punctuation into third position. Understandably the design and programming of the "Application Simulation" also feature highly. Another interesting point is the appearance of Tutorial Text - Programming ("N") in fourth spot, as this indicates inability to reproduce the text on screen from the designer's script.

Course three, designed and produced most recently, again shows similarities to the other two courses. The spelling and punctuation has in fact reduced in significance but the appearance of the programming of graphics ("H") is now a feature. Being the first "Mouse" controlled course to be monitored the appearance of comments under classification "O" was, to a certain extent, anticipated. The latest classification added to the list (ie "P" Observation Readvised) was a direct result of analysing the QA report forms and noticing the recurrence of previous comments.

Understandably an abundance of information has been produced, which renders concentrating on many areas at once, totally impracticable. We therefore prioritised the observations in terms of frequency, which allows comparisons across individual courses. This was achieved with the aid of Pareto analysis.

The overall results from course three confirm the findings in terms of priorities mentioned above (ie M,B,N,H,O,K). We were also able to focus on the observations by importance as touched on previously in the "QA report form". Each observation is categorised in terms of importance as follows:

Category 1	Critical Defect rendering release of course highly unlikely is execution error (software failure) where he course has "crashed" and needs reprogramming, or

	where some text has been incorrectly keyed which could seriously inhibit the transfer of learning.
Category 2	Major Defect making release unlikely but not impossible, ie key malfunction on one screen but fully functional elsewhere, or where a graphic does not hinder the learning but could be improved on, or difficulty in understanding how to proceed.
Category 3	Minor Defect where release is still likely if insufficient time to correct, ie spelling or punctuation error.

Each level of observation is likely to be corrected before release, but this level of importance prioritises the work involved.

The analysis of observations by category assist the QA team in identifying where to focus attention. By analysing Category I observations only, we found the top three classifications all focus on programming inaccuracies.

Many more of these charts have been produced which gives us clear indications where to concentrate our initial efforts in order to make the most impact. Another technique being investigated is that of the "cusum" chart. This refers to the cumulative sum (hence "cusum") of observations found in a sample number of screens. In essence a reference or "target value" is subtracted from each successive sample observation and the results cumulated. Values of this cumulative sum are plotted and "trend lines" are drawn on the resulting graph. If this is approximately horizontal, the value of the variable is about the same as the expected value. An overall slope downwards shows a value less than expected, and if the slope is upwards it is greater.

Another technique is that of the "cause and effect diagram" (Ishikawa) as shown in Fig.31.2, which provides an overall view of the processes that could lead towards a nonconformity report.

Improvement via communication

As mentioned, it is not possible to improve all the problems at once, so we have tended to concentrated effort on a selection of the more important and frequent observations. The improvements currently being worked on or already achieved include:

Improved reviews of designer's script. Many of the design observations should be picked up at the design review stage, as should Technical Accuracy ("L"). This would dramatically reduce the classification of observation list so that (ideally) only pure programming deficiencies remained.

Many reviewers find difficulty in visualising the paper version of text on a screen resulting in more comments when the material is later reviewed on the screen. This is being investigated by producing the pure script on screen but without the usual key functions so as to restrict comments to content, screen design and layout only.

Key Functionality - Programming ("B")

If the above were successful, much more could be achieved in this area by further developing tools such as "Fault Tree Analysis" (FTA's) which would help to pinpoint exactly why a programmer was allowing inaccuracies. It could be inexperience, lack of time, insufficient testing, etc.

The creation of a "shell" for navigation purposes will standardise the process, and significantly reduce this classification without stifling design. Many courses are now becoming "Windows" based, and the use of the recorder function in "Windows" allows selected key presses to be automatically remembered and reproduced on demand. This encourages a more efficient testing process to be maintained, thereby increasing the speed of course release.

Spelling and Punctuation ("K")

This has been improved in recent courses by using a programming language that is able to import the designer's script thereby cutting the keying-in process by half.

These has been improved in recent courses by using a programming language that is able to import the designer's script thereby cutting the keying-in process by half.

These improvements are only likely through effective communication and a willingness to improve. It is up to QA to identify, analyse, encourage, support and coach so that both the training provided and the method of producing that training are, and continue to be of the highest quality.

Index